I0485262

Table of Contents

I. Introduction 1
II. Justice for the Violators of the Laws of War 4
III. The Seeds of International Justice – World War II International Military Tribunals 8
    A. IMT 10
        1. Stated Goals of the IMT 11
        2. Charter & Duration 14
        3. Tribunal Composition & Procedures 16
            a. Tribunal Composition 16
            b. Tribunal Procedure 20
        4. Perceived Fairness of the IMT at Nuremberg 24
        5. Role of Court as Part of Larger Reconstruction Plan. 27
        6. Were the stated goals accomplished? 29
    B. IMTFE 31
        1. Stated Goals of the IMTFE 32
        2. Charter & Duration 38
        3. Tribunal Composition & Procedure 39
            a. Tribunal Composition 40
            b. Tribunal Procedure 41
        4. Perceived Fairness of the IMTFE 44
        5. Role of the Court as Part of Larger Reconstruction Plan 48
        6. Were the stated goals accomplished? 48
IV. The Use of National Military Commissions for the Prosecution of War Criminals 49
    A. Effectiveness of US Military Commissions for the Prosecution of War Criminals 52
        1. United States Commissions in Germany 53
        2. United States Commissions in the Pacific 58
    B. British Prosecutions Before Military Commissions 62
        1. British Commissions in Germany 65
        2. British Commissions in the Pacific 68
    C. Perceptions of Fairness and Lessons Learned from the World War II Commissions ... 74
V. The Overarching Goals of Reconciliation & Restoration of Peace 77
    A. Post-Conflict Reconciliation and the Long Term Restoration of Peace 77
    B. Domestic Reconciliation: Lessons Learned from South Africa? 80
    C. Modern Trend: Universal Jurisdiction as a Legalistic Threat to Future Stability 85
    D. Modern Trend: The Special Court of Sierra Leone – Positive Prequel for the Future . 88
VI. Retooling the Past: A new dock for modern war criminals 93
    A. Iraq's Multicultural Face 94
    B. Borrowing from the Past & Present – Justice in Post-Conflict Iraq 100
        1. The International Military Tribunal – Iraq 103
        2. National Military Commissions 108
        3. Domestic Courts 110
        4. Truth and Reconciliation Commission 112
    C. The International Control Council - Iraq 116

    1. The International Control Council and Prisoner of War Repatriation..................... 118
    2. The International Control Council and the Implementation of International Norms
.... 120
    3. The International Control Council, Competing Jurisdiction and Appeals............... 122
VII. Conclusion... 125

Among free peoples who possess equality before the law we must cultivate an affable temper and what is called loftiness of spirit.[1]

I. Introduction

The history of Europe is a history of war. Mongols[2], Huns[3], Moors[4], Turks[5], Romans[6] and modern Europeans have fought and died throughout Europe for control of the continent. Japan knew a similar culture in which war and its practitioners held a venerated position in a society antithetical to democratic principles and the rule of law. These societies gave birth to two of the most efficient war machines of history: Adolf Hitler's Germany and Emperor Hirohito's Imperial Japan. United, Germany and Japan along with their lesser Axis Allies waged a war of conquest that spread to all of the populated continents. The United States

---

[1] CICERO, ON DUTIES 35 (M.T. Griffith & E.M. Atkins, trans., Cambridge 1991).

[2] J.F.C. FULLER, I A MILITARY HISTORY OF THE WESTERN WORLD 283 (1954).

[3] *Id.* at 282.

[4] The wars between the Christian Spanish and the Muslim Moors of predominately Berber and Arabic descent battled for the control of Spain beginning in 912. The Moors held onto various amounts of Spain until their ultimate defeat at Grenada in 1492. GEORGE C. KOHN, DICTIONARY OF WARS 437-39 (1987).

[5] A particularly bloody series of engagements occurred in Transylvania beginning in 1657 when the Transylvanians unsuccessfully attempted to throw off the rule of their Turkish overlords. *Id.* at 470.

[6] There are countless books written over the ages of various Roman conquests throughout Europe and the signs of Roman conquest and occupation dot the landscapes of Europe. For a Roman account of some of the civilizations with which the Romans waged war, *see generally,* TACITUS, GERMANIA (J.B. Rives, Trans., Clarendon 1999) (c. 69).

and her Allies found themselves in a struggle for national survival in the face of a powerful coalition bent on world conquest.

Though all wars expose its participants to unique horrors, World War II brought the world atrocities of historic proportions. Jews were murdered by the millions throughout Europe in furtherance of Hitler's master plan of a Europe purged of what he deemed, for example, to be racially inferior stock. In addition, Japanese soldiers visited horrors upon captured soldiers that often included execution, decapitation of the dead and cannibalism. The Japanese Government created corps of foreign sexual slaves for the wanton use of their armed forces.

Yet, today it is difficult to imagine a modern war between the United States, Germany and Japan. Western Europe has known its longest period of peace in its long and bloody history. Japan, has transitioned to democracy, shed its militant culture, and notwithstanding its recent economic setbacks, remains one of the most efficient and robust economies on earth.[7] On the strategic front, Germany sits with the United States as an equal voting member at NATO, and serves with American troops in combat operations abroad. Japan is a key American ally in the Pacific.

---

[7] Recent research has sought to identify the most competitive countries. The research focused upon factors such as their public institutions, macroeconomic environment and level of technology. On this list the United States holds the first position but Japan comes in at 13, close behind the United Kingdom and solidly ahead of Hong Kong. *Competitiveness Rankings,* THE ECONOMIST, Nov. 16, 2002, at 98. As discussed *infra* notes 188 – 191 and accompanying text, much of the post war successes of Japan can be attributed to the success of the goals of the occupation of Japan.

This dramatic shift can provide lessons to help secure the successful resolution of hostilities in tomorrow's wars. There were many factors that set the stage for a series of successful transitions. These transitions were first from war to peace, followed by cooperation in the reconstruction, and ultimately a transition toward a political and economic alliance. The reestablishment and the development of respect for the rule of law and democracy in Germany and Japan was of paramount importance to the process of the reconciliation of the former belligerents and their transformation into future Allies.

Against this backdrop, this paper will examine the role that the various systems of justice played in the ultimate reconciliation of the belligerents of World War II. From this standard, modern jurisprudential trends for the prosecution of war criminals will be evaluated. Section II will provide an overview of the goals of the traditional American justice system as compared to those of international and national systems of justice used to prosecute violators of the laws of war and or other crimes susceptible to post conflict prosecution by the international community. Section III will analyze the goals, procedures and effectiveness of the international military tribunals created for the prosecution of war criminals in the wake of World War II. Section IV will provide a similar analysis for the use of national courts and commissions to try those who violate the laws of war. Sections III and IV will also include a discussion of the effectiveness of the studied systems and highlight lessons learned from the experience. Section V will focus on the important goal of reconciliation as a key aspect that should be incorporated into any system of justice that is established after the cessation of hostilities.

Based on this background, section VI will propose a system of justice for the prosecution for Iraqi war criminals[8] apprehended after the liberation of Iraq. This proposal will leverage the lessons of the past with the aim of developing a system of justice for war criminals that contributes to the prospects for a lasting peace and the reconciliation of the various domestic and international parties.[9] This proposal is based upon a philosophy that any system of post-conflict justice for war criminals must serve the ultimate ends of peace and reconciliation. And though the process should include the punishment of the wrongdoer, the process used to achieve these ends must be carefully tailored to the situation. Further, efforts must be undertaken to establish legitimacy and transparency. Transparency serves to build confidence in the outcome, and, critically, to provide the local population with immediate insight into the rule of law in action.

II. Justice for the Violators of the Laws of War

---

[8] This paper presents a proposed solution for the punishment of those who committed acts that can be broadly defined as war crimes up until the moment of regime change. Crimes that are committed after the occupation would be prosecuted in occupation courts or Iraqi domestic courts as they are reopened after occupation. As will be discussed *infra* at notes 363-364 and accompanying text, as the organs of occupation slowly turn authority back to the reconstructed domestic authorities, the systems may begin to merge to some degree with respect to actors which are not "major war criminals." The acts that define crimes under international law are most often cognizable in domestic courts as well. While killing thousands may be the crime of genocide under international law, such acts amount to a like number of counts of murder to a domestic court. The punishment is often the same.

[9] For the purposes of this paper, reconciliation is a social and political process that through various means serves to reduce the hostilities that existed between the international belligerents and may exist between components of a diverse domestic population. This paper will seek to illuminate the important contribution that the system of justice developed for war criminals in a post conflict environment can make to the ultimate reconciliation of the belligerents.

American jurisprudence recognizes numerous theories for bringing those that violate criminal laws to justice. These theories include: punishment of the wrongdoer;[10] rehabilitation of the wrongdoer; protection of society from the wrongdoer; specific deterrence of the wrongdoer, and general deterrence of the class of wrongdoer in question.[11] To this list of motivations, military courts add the goal of the preservation of good order and discipline in the armed forces.[12]

These goals are equally important considerations when seeking the prosecution and punishment of those who violate the laws of war. Circumstances surrounding the prosecution of war criminals, however, may require the addition of goals that eclipse those sought by traditional systems of justice. These goals include complementing and encouraging the respect for the rule of law, the encouragement of democratization and the ultimate reconciliation of the belligerents. Consideration of these goals is crucial in developing the appropriate international forums for the prosecution of war criminals. Further, in some cases these ultimate goals may overshadow the traditional purposes of the criminal justice system.[13]

---

[10] Punishment of the wrongdoer as an appropriate basis for a goal of a criminal justice system has been developed by American philosopher Jeffrey Murphy who advocates a "retributive punishment theory" that seeks to use punishment as a method "to put burdens and benefits back into balance." *See* MICHAEL TONRY, SENTENCING MATTERS 17 (1996).

[11] ABA STANDARDS FOR CRIMINAL JUSTICE SENTENCING 18-2.1(a)(i-v) (3d ed. 1994).

[12] U.S. DEP'T OF ARMY, PAM. 27-9, MILITARY JUDGES BENCHBOOK para. 8-3-21 (1 Apr. 2001).

[13] For example, as discussed *infra* at notes 365-370 and accompanying text, it may at times be necessary to offer non-punitive resolutions to those who have committed serious violations of law in order to preserve the legitimacy of the justice system and to further the reconciliation of the former belligerents. An example is when the volume of potential accused far outweigh the ability of the system of justice to prosecute them all. This

"War Criminal"[14] is an imprecise term that became synonymous with a broad class of wrongdoer during the International Military Tribunals[15] (IMTs) of World War II. Misconduct prosecuted before these tribunals fell into the three broad categories. They were crimes against peace,[16] war crimes,[17] and crimes against humanity.[18] Personal jurisdiction, however, was severely limited by both the Tokyo and Nuremberg IMTs in that they were limited to only "major" violators. As will be discussed herein, this limited scope contributed to the effective contribution of the IMTs toward the overall post-war goals of the Allies.[19]

By design, the limited scope of the IMTs left a vacuum which was to be filled by both national military commissions and domestic prosecutions through local civilian courts.[20] These courts and commissions afforded individual nations the opportunity to try cases

---

paper will argue that in such circumstances a non-punitive truth and reconciliation commission would be preferable to process and fix accountability for those whose conduct is less severe than the key perpetrators of crime. This, in the author's opinion, is preferable to a system when confronted with overwhelming criminal activity simply opts to randomly prosecute some while ignoring others without consistent procedures.

[14] For the purposes of this article, unless otherwise specified, the term "war criminal" shall be used to refer to offenders whose conduct fell within the jurisdiction of the International Military Tribunal at Nuremberg. As this paper will discuss, the IMTs at Nuremberg and Tokyo were limited to cases involving "major" war criminals who engaged in one of three classes of prohibited conduct. The conduct over which the IMTs were seized of jurisdiction was: crimes against the peace; war crimes; and crimes against humanity. CHARTER OF THE INTERNATIONAL MILITARY TRIBUNAL art. 6(a-c), *reprinted in* DEP'T ST. PUB. 2420, TRIAL OF WAR CRIMINALS 15 (1945) [hereinafter IMT CHARTER].

[15] In the aftermath of World War II, International Military Tribunals (IMTs) were established in Nuremberg and Tokyo. *See infra* notes 39-116 and accompanying text and *infra* notes 117-191 and accompanying text, respectively.

[16] IMT CHARTER, supra note 14, art. 6(a).

[17] *Id.* art. 6(b).

[18] *Id.* art. 6(c).

[19] *See infra* notes 145-146 and accompanying text.

[20] This vacuum was created by limiting the scope of the IMT to major war criminals which in practice was limited to the highest civilian and military leaders of Nazi Germany.

important to their citizens such as when their soldiers had been victimized by wrongdoers

below the scope of the jurisdiction of an IMT. Likewise, national courts and commissions

pursued war criminals and saboteurs in the country in which the crimes were committed.

Opponents of *ad hoc* systems argue that such tribunals and military commissions are too

inefficient for effective international justice.[21] Further, they note that some jurisdictions

because of political reasons or a poorly developed legal system may fail to bring lesser war

criminals to justice though within their reach.[22] Because of such concerns, there has been a

rise in the interest of standing tribunals with prospective jurisdiction leading to the

International Criminal Court (ICC), and greater support for the concept of universal

jurisdiction.[23] These two approaches, however, do not provide for an effective solution for

Iraq, and as discussed below, both of these movements should be rejected. Many of the

arguments in favor of these methods of justice appear justified when analyzed within the

limited framework of the traditional goals of a criminal justice system.[24] However, the ICC

---

[21] For a general criticism of problems related to ad hoc tribunals with suggestions for improvement focused on the ICTR, *see generally* Todd Howland & William Calathes, *The U.N.'s International Criminal Tribunal, Is It Justice or Jingoism for Rwanda? A Call for Transformation*, 39 VA. J. INT'L L. 135 (1998).

[22] *See, e.g.*, Walter Gary Sharp, Jr., *International Obligations to Search for and Arrest War Criminals: Government Failure in the Former Yugoslavia?*, 7 DUKE J. COMP. & INT'L L. 411 (1997).

[23] Universal jurisdiction can be defined narrowly as that which "provides every nation with jurisdiction over certain crimes recognized universally, regardless of the place of the offense or of the nationalities of the offender or the victims." Jon B. Jordan, *Universal Jurisdiction in a Dangerous World: A Weapon for all Nations Against International Crime*, 9 MSU-DCL J. INT'L L. 1, 3 (2000).

[24] *See supra* notes 10-12 and accompanying text.

and the expansive use of universal jurisdiction can serve to undercut the overarching goals of restoration of peace and reconciliation of the belligerents in a post-armed conflict situation.[25]

For practical and legal reasons, the International Criminal Court will not be available for the prosecution of war criminals apprehended in Iraq in the wake of a regime change.[26] Further, any efforts by third parties to rely on national courts outside of Iraq to prosecute wrongdoers under a theory of universal jurisdiction would provide an incomplete solution at best.[27] Post conflict Iraq should include a system of international justice that utilizes an international military tribunal complemented by national commissions conducted in Iraq and eventually by reestablished Iraqi domestic forums.[28] This is a daunting task without an off the shelf solution. Any efforts in this area require a careful evaluation of the procedures of the past and consideration of the lessons learned.

III. The Seeds of International Justice – World War II International Military Tribunals.

Iraq, unfortunately, is not the first country in the modern era to bring war to its neighbors and terror to its people. The Allied powers of World War II were confronted with atrocities

---

[25] *See infra* notes 305-307 and accompanying text.

[26] Iraq has not signed or ratified the Statute of Rome. Rome Statute of the International Criminal Court, U.N. Doc. A/CONF. 183/9 (1998) (United Nations Diplomatic Conference of Plenipotentiaries on the Establishment of an International Criminal Court, July 17, 1998), *reprinted in* 37 I.L.M. 998 (1998) [hereinafter Rome Statute].

[27] Such exercise of jurisdiction by nations with little direct interest in the conflict could serve to damage the reconstruction of Iraq by injecting an unnecessary political process into a destabilized environment. Further, practical problems such as location of evidence and witnesses and competing needs for the same by courts operating within Iraq in a post-conflict environment would further detract from any benefit that such extraterritorial forums might provide.

[28] *See infra* notes 343-370 and accompanying text.

of an unprecedented nature directed at soldiers, civilians and the very fabric of society. Yet no court of an international composition existed to bring the wrongdoers to justice. Further, it was the subject of much debate as to whether such a tribunal was necessary or even legal. Prime Minister Winston Churchill questioned the need to try any of the major war criminals that he referred to as "arch-criminals" under the theory that it was legally justified to summarily execute them upon identification.[29] Others questioned the legitimacy of attempting to find criminal conduct behind the horrors and fog of war.[30] At Nuremberg, all defense counsel joined in a unified challenge of the underlying legitimacy of the International Military Tribunal by invoking the legal maxim *"nulla poena sine lege."*[31]

Rallying under this banner, these defense counsel attacked the legitimacy of the IMT and highlighted the irony of the use of what was perceived as an *ex post facto* scheme of justice. In the words of the defense:

> The present Trial can, therefore, as far as Crimes against the Peace shall be avenged, not invoke existing international law, it is rather a proceeding pursuant to a new penal law, a penal law enacted only after the crime. This is repugnant to a principle of jurisprudence sacred to the civilized world, the partial violation of which by Hitler's Germany has been vehemently discountenanced outside and inside the Reich. This principle is to the effect that only he can be punished who offended against a law in existence at the time of the commission of the act . . . . This

---

[29] TELFORD TAYLOR, THE ANATOMY OF THE NUREMBERG TRIALS 34 (1992).

[30] *See infra* notes 102-104 and accompanying text.

[31] "No punishment without a law authorizing it." BLACK'S LAW DICTIONARY 1095 (7th ed. 1999).

maxim is one of the great fundamental principles [of the
Signatories to the Charter of the IMT.][32]

The Tribunal rejected this argument and ignored the defense request to seek guidance

from "recognized authorities on international law."[33] In reaching its decision, the Tribunal

found that the Charter was created under the "sovereign legislative power by the countries to

which the German Reich unconditionally surrendered."[34] Further, the Tribunal relied on its

status as an organ of the occupying powers as a basis for exercising sovereignty over the

defendants, and not as a means to arbitrarily mete out punishment by "victorious Nations."[35]

The Tribunal held that the defense misapplied the maxim *"Nullum crimen sine lege, nulla*

poena sine lege"[36] by misconstruing it as a restriction on "sovereignty."[37] The Tribunal held

that the acts were known to be unlawful at the time of the act and thus not *ex post facto*, and

that the use of the Tribunal was a proper exercise of sovereignty in light of the unconditional

surrender of the parties.[38]

A. IMT

---

[32] Motion Adopted by all Defense Counsel, 1 I.M.T. 168 (1945).

[33] *Id.* at 170. Rather than moving the court to grant the relief requested, the defense requested the IMT to seek counsel from international law scholars before rendering an opinion.

[34] Judgment, 1 I.M.T. 171, 218 (1946).

[35] *Id.*

[36] Though not included in BLACK'S LAW DICTIONARY, it translates to mean "No crime without law, no punishment without a law authorizing it."

[37] Judgment, 1 I.M.T. 171, 219 (1946).

[38] *Id.* at 218-19.

Law is a common consciousness of obligation.[39]

As discussed above, the International Military Tribunal at Nuremberg (IMT) was the first international tribunal of its kind to punish wrongdoers for acts that were committed prior to the inception of the court. To gauge its effectiveness, it is necessary to evaluate the goals of the Tribunal, its Charter, jurisdiction, composition and the role the IMT played as part of the overall reconstruction plan of the Allies. Such a review reveals that the IMT provided a procedurally fair system of justice that served both the immediate needs of a criminal justice system while complementing the reconstruction plan of the Allies. Most importantly, the success of the IMT contributed greatly to the "package of justice" resources, which furthered the ends of ultimate reconciliation of the belligerents.

1. Stated Goals of the IMT

To enable its goals to be achieved, the IMT at Nuremberg first sought to establish its legitimacy amid broad diversity of opinion. This legitimacy rested on "the proposition that international penal law is judicially enforceable law, and that it therefore may and should be enforced by criminal process . . . . [this] basic proposition is not purely or even primarily American, but of rather cosmopolitan origin."[40] Exercise of this criminal process over the Nazis rested on the principle that the perpetrators of the "unjust" war would no longer be able

---

[39] KENZO TAKAYANAGI, THE TOKYO TRIALS AND INTERNATIONAL LAW 1 (1948). Kenzo Takayangi was a defense counsel before the IMTFE and delivered a response to the Prosecution's arguments based upon international law at the Tribunal.

[40] TELFORD TAYLOR, FINAL REPORT TO THE SECRETARY OF THE ARMY ON THE NUERNBERG WAR CRIMES TRIALS UNDER CONTROL COUNCIL LAW NO. 10 1 (1949) [hereinafter FINAL REPORT].

to shield their combatants with "the mantle of protection around acts which otherwise would be crimes" except when pursued as part of a just war.[41]

Further, the Allied powers announced two years before the end of World War II that Axis soldiers and leaders guilty of committing atrocities would be prosecuted thus placing them on notice of the fate that might await them.[42] Collectively, the embryonic group that would form the seeds of the United Nations announced that those who committed "war crimes should stand trial."[43] Upon this platform of legitimacy, the IMT sought to consolidate the fragmented sources of international law that provided the bases for individual criminal responsibility.

The IMT sought to accomplish its stated goal of a "just and prompt trial and punishment of the major war criminals of the European Axis,"[44] but through this process a higher goal was undertaken. In the words of United States Supreme Court Associate Justice Robert H. Jackson,[45] "now we have the concrete application of these abstractions in a way which ought

---

[41] REPORT OF ROBERT H. JACKSON TO THE PRESIDENT, RELEASED BY THE WHITE HOUSE ON JUNE 7, 1945 *reprinted in* DEP'T OF ST. PUB. 2420, TRIAL OF THE WAR CRIMINALS 1, 8 (1945).

[42] The Triparte Conference at Moscow, Oct. 19-30, 1943, *reprinted* in International Conciliation, No. 395, at 599-605 (1943) [hereinafter Moscow Declaration]. In the days leading up to the beginning of hostilities in Iraq, similar pronouncements were made by the United States government. Michael Kirkland, *U.S. Plans Iraqi trials*, WASH. TIMES (Jan. 8, 2003), *available at* http://www.washtimes.com/upi-breaking/20030108-011244-9167r.htm.

[43] TELFORD TAYLOR, THE ANATOMY OF THE NUREMBERG TRIALS 26 (1992).

[44] IMT CHARTER, *supra* note 14, art. 1.

[45] Associate Justice Robert Jackson was designated by President Harry Truman as the U. S. Representative and Chief Counsel for the US Delegation to the IMT. As such, he directed the prosecutions efforts and served as the Chief Prosecutor at the IMT for the United States. Scott W. Johnson & John H. Hinderaker, *Guidelines for Cross-Examination: Lessons Learned from the Cross-Examination of Hermann Goering*, 59 BENCH & B. OF MINN. (October 2002), *at* http://www2.mnbar.org/benchandbar/2002/oct02/cross-exam.htm.

to make clear to the world that those who lead their nations into aggressive war face individual accountability for such acts."[46] The framers of the Charter of the International Military Tribunal sought to ensure that the procedures would be perceived as fair and thus serve to legitimize the outcomes of the trials.

In approaching the problem of developing a Charter that would meet these ends, the Allied powers pulled from multiple civilian and military legal traditions including the United States, Great Britain, France and the Soviet Union.[47] Those charged with developing the Charter and procedures of the IMT recognized the difficulty of blending the common law and continental legal systems of the Allied powers to reach a coherent product agreeable to the parties.[48] Notwithstanding the difficulties, the drafters of the IMT Charter understood that the creation of a workable product was critical if legitimacy was to be established. Justice Jackson noted that he thought "that the world would be infinitely poorer if we were to

---

[46] Statement by Justice Jackson on War Trials Agreement (August 12, 1945), *available at* http://www.yale.edu/lawweb/avalon/imt/jack02.htm.

[47] These countries brought different concepts of the extent to which the use of military tribunals were deemed appropriate prior to World War II. For example, the United States had traditionally limited the scope and duration of military tribunals and commissions to periods when military operations effectively closed the civilian courts as established in *Ex Parte Mulligan*, 71 U.S. (4 Wall.) 1, 2 (1866). Great Britain, however, upon entry into World War II had a legal tradition that permitted even the trial of civilians before military courts when the civilian courts were still open and functioning. Frederick Bernays Wiener, A PRACTICAL MANUAL OF MARTIAL LAW 131 (1940). It is of note that while Brigadier General Telford Taylor was concerned about ultimately shifting responsibility for trials of war criminals back to the German domestic courts, the Charter of the IMT was silent as to this.

[48] Justice Robert Jackson, Statement by Justice Jackson on War Trials Agreement (August 12, 1945), *available at* http://www.yale.edu/lawweb/avalon/imt/jack2.htm.

confess that the nations which now dominate the western world hold ideas of justice so irreconcilable that no common procedure could be devised or carried out."[49]

2. Charter & Duration

When analyzing the fairness and effectiveness of the Charter of the IMT it is critical to consider its limited scope. Unlike modern *ad hoc* tribunals that often purport to exercise jurisdiction over any war criminal of any stripe,[50] the IMT was strictly limited to bad actors that met two threshold requirements. First, they must have been members of the European Axis.[51] Further, they must have been "major war criminals."[52] Such a limited exercise of jurisdiction helped to minimize claims of selective prosecution while providing the world community the opportunity to collectively seek justice from those most responsible for German atrocities. Further, lesser actors were not permitted to escape justice, but were relegated to other forums such as national military commissions or domestic courts.[53]

---

[49] *Id.*

[50] The breadth of the ICTY charter has opened it up to continuing criticism as a political organ as opposed to a fair system of justice. Surveys of Serbian public opinion indicate that they do not believe the Tribunal as just, but simply a "politically biased and anti-Serb court." Peter Ford, *Serbs still ignore role in atrocity*, THE CHRISTIAN SCI. MONITOR (Feb. 11 2002), *available at* http://www.csmonitor.com/2002/0211/p01s02-woeu.html.

[51] IMT CHARTER, *supra* note 14, art. 1.

[52] *Id.*

[53] Efforts to reduce the perception of a selective or inconsistent system of justice was also a key concern for planners of military commissions after WWII. *See infra* notes 266-269 and accompanying text.

The duration of the IMT was not defined in the Charter. Article 22 refers to the Tribunal

as having a "permanent seat"[54] in Nuremberg though it is clear that the parties did not intend

to maintain a continuous presence even as some major war criminals remained at large. The

position of the United States was that the IMT would not be reactivated in the event of the

future apprehension of a major war criminal, though its Charter permitted reactivation.[55] The

IMT was to serve its function during the period of occupation of Germany, but as Germany

demilitarized it was envisioned that its domestic courts would begin to play a role in the

prosecution of war criminals to be supplemented by Allied military courts as necessary.[56] In

the words of Brigadier General Telford Taylor in his report to the Secretary of the Army:

minor actors "should be brought to trial on criminal charges before German tribunals."[57]

Further, he cautioned President Truman against considering convening additional cases

before the IMT "at this late stage."[58]

---

[54] IMT CHARTER, *supra* note 14, art. 22.

[55] Though the French demonstrated a desire to have a second trial before the IMT, the United States rejected this finding that national commissions and occupation courts were sufficient for the remaining cases at hand. As such, no other cases were convened before the IMT. *See* TELFORD TAYLOR, FINAL REPORT TO THE SECRETARY OF THE ARMY ON THE NUERNBERG WAR CRIMES TRIALS UNDER CONTROL COUNCIL LAW NO. 10 27 (1949).

[56] It is important to note that before the end of World War II the British were concerned about the over expansion of the jurisdiction of what they referred to as "Mixed Military Tribunals" for the prosecution of war criminals. The British preferred the use of national courts, and considered the use of an International Military Tribunals "with cases which for one reason or another could not be tried in national courts . . . to include those cases where a person is accused of having committed war crimes against the nationals of several of the United Nations." Memorandum to President Roosevelt from the Secretaries of State and War and the Attorney General (Jan. 22, 1945), *reprinted at*, DEP'T OF ST. PUB 3080, REPORT OF ROBERT H. JACKSON, UNITED STATES REPRESENTATIVE TO THE INTERNATIONAL CONFERENCE ON MILITARY TRIALS 3, 8 [hereinafter INTERNATIONAL CONFERENCE REPORT].

[57] TELFORD TAYLOR, FINAL REPORT TO THE SECRETARY OF THE ARMY ON THE NUERNBERG WAR CRIMES TRIALS UNDER CONTROL COUNCIL LAW NO. 10, 95 (1949).

[58] General Taylor provided this advice to President Truman in 1949. *Id.*

The decision to limit the time for the prosecution of war criminals before the IMT served

important policy goals. First was the desire to reestablish the rule of law and legitimate

domestic authority within Germany. As these systems were reestablished, the increased

reliance on German courts served to further the overall goals of reconstruction. Second, it

facilitated the reconciliation of the former belligerents by bringing an end to one of the final

formal processes of Allied military activity in Germany. This process served as an important

bridge from the final judicial extensions of war to the reemergence of civil society in

Germany.

3. Tribunal Composition & Procedures

a. Tribunal Composition

The signatories that created the IMT – the United States, Great Britain, the Provisional

Government of the French Republic, and the Soviet Union[59] – were represented at all times[60]

at the IMT. A nation's appointed representative or his alternate was always present during

the proceedings.[61] This enforced cross-sectional representation furthered the goal of

---

[59] AGREEMENT FOR THE ESTABLISHMENT OF AN INTERNATIONAL MILITARY TRIBUNAL art. 7 (1945), *reprinted in* DEP'T OF ST. PUB 2420, TRIAL OF WAR CRIMINALS 13 [hereinafter IMT AGREEMENT].

[60] IMT CHARTER, *supra* note 14, art. 2. As discussed herein, this is one of the areas in which the IMT differed substantially from the IMTFE. *See infra* notes 155-157 and accompanying text.

[61] IMT CHARTER, *supra* note 14, art. 4(a).

establishing legitimacy, both in theory and practice. The Judgment[62] of the IMT revealed that the representatives brought their own independent notions of justice to the proceedings.

The diverging opinions of the IMT representatives can be seen in the twenty-three page dissent filed by the Soviet judge to the Judgment. This dissent represented a stark divide between the Soviet representative and the other Allied powers represented at the IMT. The split in opinion of the representatives stemmed from their willingness to extend the jurisdiction of the Court and to punish those brought before it. Further, it echoed many of the debates surrounding the use of its purported retroactive jurisdiction.[63] Notably, the Soviet representative Major General (Jurisprudence) I. T. Nikitchenko was critical of the Tribunal's Judgment that passed down three acquittals, spared the life of Defendant Rudolf Hess, and refused to extend collective criminal responsibility to the Reich Cabinet or the General Staff.[64]

This divergence of opinion among the jurists served to legitimize the procedures utilized by the Tribunal. First, it demonstrated that the Tribunal was more than "victor's justice" as it illuminated core divergences in international opinion as to the scope of imputed criminal responsibility. While a tribunal focused upon meting out victor's justice would be expected

---

[62] The final verdict of guilt and the subsequent sentences announced are referred to by the IMT as its "Judgment."

[63] *See supra* notes 31-38 and accompanying text.

[64] The Soviet member described the acquittals as "unfounded" developing his argument for conviction on theories of guilt by association. For example, he felt that the uncontroverted evidence that Defendant Schacht *"consciously and deliberately supported the Nazi Party and actively aided in the seizure of power in Germany."* Dissenting Opinion of the Soviet Member of the International Military Tribunal, 1 I.M.T. 342, 343 (1946) (emphasis in original).

to expand its substantive jurisdiction to the fullest extent possible, the debate and divergence of opinion reflect that this did not occur at the IMT. Second, this divergence ensured that the Judgment handed down at Nuremberg reflected a consensus among nations with vastly different legal systems. This consensus helped to ensure a more conservative evaluation of the state international law with respect to criminal responsibility for actions taken on behalf of or at the direction of the sovereign during war.[65]

This consensus required the reconciliation of competing legal systems as well as divergent political philosophies. These structural and philosophical differences complicated the development of the IMT, but served to ensure a check on the expansion of international criminal responsibility beyond legitimacy. The acquittal of defendant Hjalmar Schacht highlights such a point. Schacht's acquittal did not reflect a lack of consensus on the facts. His acquittal reflected a debate about the scope of international criminal responsibility and the degree that the actions of one could be tied to the actions of another absent strong evidence.[66]

Defendant Schacht began his affiliation with the Nazi Party while he served as the Commissioner of Currency and as the President of the Reichsbank.[67] After the Nazis came to power, Schacht enjoyed a period of favor through much of the pre-war period and held

---

[65] The dissent in the Judgment reflects a fundamental rift between the states represented on the Tribunal that had the greatest respect for individual rights and that of the USSR that was by its nature and charter the most collectivist. Some modern historians see this as a rift between elements of Europe and the United States that began early in the twentieth century and continues today. *See* PAUL JOHNSON, MODERN TIMES: FROM THE TWENTIES TO THE NINETIES 271-76 (1991).

[66] *See infra* notes 74-76 and accompanying text.

[67] Judgment, 1 I.M.T. 171, 307 (1946).

numerous key positions within the government. Of greatest note, he served as the Plenipotentiary General for War Economy from 1935 through 1937.[68] In this capacity, under the authority of a secret German law enacted on May 21, 1935, he held the power "to issue legal orders, deviating from existing laws . . . [and was the] responsible head for financing wars through the Reich Ministry and the Reichsbank."[69] Though Schacht held other positions of responsibility within the Reich after 1937, this was the highest position he held until imprisoned in 1944 under suspicion of involvement in an assassination attempt on Adolf Hitler.[70]

In light of Schacht's involvement in the central banking operations that provided the hard currency necessary for Hitler's war time aggression, he was indicted by the Tribunal as being part of the "Common Plan or Conspiracy"[71] that "involved the common plan or conspiracy to commit . . . Crimes against Peace, War Crimes, and Crimes against Humanity . . . ."[72] Further, he was indicted for crimes against the peace.[73] The facts underlying the findings of

---

[68] *Id.*

[69] Dissenting Opinion of the Soviet Member of the International Military Tribunal, 1 I.M.T. 342, 344 (1946).

[70] Judgment, 1 I.M.T. 171, 310 (1946).

[71] *Id.* at 29.

[72] *Id.*

[73] *Id. at* 42. Participation in a "common plan or conspiracy" related to the active participation in a plan to wage a war of aggression "in violation of international treaties, agreements or assurances." *Id.* at 29. Similarly, "crimes against peace" were limited to "planning, preparation, initiation, and waging wars of aggression, which were also in violation of international treaties, agreements and assurances." *Id.* at 42 The indictment specifically limited such actions further to Poland, the United Kingdom and France in 1939, the Netherlands and Luxembourg in 1940, and Yugoslavia, Greece, the USSR, and the United States in 1941. *Id.* "War Crimes" focused on waging "total war" in a manner that included "methods of combat and of military occupation in direct conflict with the laws and customs of war, and the commission of crimes perpetrated [against] armies, prisoners of war, and . . . against civilians." *Id.* at 43. "Crimes against humanity" primarily

the Tribunal and the dissent of the Soviet representative were fundamentally the same. The key distinction, however, was the extent to which the majority was willing to impute knowledge "beyond a reasonable doubt" to an actor who at times appeared more concerned with the impact that Hitler's procurement practices might have on monetary inflation than on the amount of materiel available to Hitler's war machine.[74] The Soviet dissent seems more willing to base a conviction on guilt by association[75] and being a bad man.[76]

b. Tribunal Procedure

The development of the Charter of the International Military Tribunal was fraught with difficulties. The source of these difficulties was the divergence of the legal and political philosophies of the countries represented. Prime Minister Churchill's belief that major war criminals should be subject to summary execution upon identification[77] represents the thinnest of procedural protections for an accused and marked the most extreme position

---

focused on murder and other acts of violence targeted at those "who were suspected of being hostile to the Nazi Party and all who were . . . opposed to the common plan [of the Nazis]." *Id.* at 65.

[74] Though undoubtedly a bad actor, Schacht never seemed to get quite with the entire "conquer the world" program of the Third Reich. During 1939 when Hitler was concerned about waging a war on multiple fronts with some of the most powerful nations on Earth, Schacht submitted a detailed memorandum to Hitler urging him to "reduce expenditures for armaments" and strive for a "balanced budget as the only method of preventing inflation." Judgment, 1 I.M.T. 171, 308-09 (1946).

[75] *See* Dissenting Opinion of the Soviet Member of the International Military Tribunal, 1 I.M.T. 342, 342-48 (1946).

[76] Though the crime of being a "bad man" was not recognized by the IMT as a basis for punishment, the "bad man" concept in one form or another as a basis of punishment did enjoy a renaissance in military justice circles during the nineteenth century for crimes committed during war. For an excellent discussion of the criminal jurisprudence of bad men such as the "jayhawker," "armed prowler" and other war time ruffians, *see* Major William E. Boyle, Jr., *Under the Black Flag: Execution and Retaliation in Mosby's Confederacy*, 144 MIL. L. REV. 148 (1994).

[77] *See supra* note 29 and accompanying text.

considered by the Allies. There were also marked differences between the Soviets and the United States regarding key provisions of the Charter. Of note is a comparison of the final Soviet and American draft proposals as to the procedures of the Tribunal as it related to the rights of the accused.

Though never implemented, the proposed Soviet model for the rights of the accused was incorporated into Article 22 of the Last Draft of the Soviet Statute styled "Rights of Defendants and Provisions for the Promptness of Trial "[78] and Article 24 entitled "Defense."[79] Soviet draft Article 22 in its entirety provides:

> The trial while ensuring the rightful interests of the defendants must at the same time be based on principles which will ensure the prompt carrying out of justice. All attempts to use trial for Nazi propaganda and for attacks on the Allied countries should be decisively ruled out.[80]

These "rights" were followed with further imprecise guidance in Soviet draft Article 24 which provides in its pertinent part that the "right of the defendant to defence shall be recognized. Duly authorized lawyers or other persons admitted by the Tribunal shall plead for the defendant at his request."[81]

---

[78] Last Draft of Soviet Statute (1945), *reprinted at* INTERNATIONAL CONFERENCE REPORT, *supra* note 56, at 167, 178.

[79] *Id.* at 179.

[80] *Id* at 178.

[81] *Id.* at 179.

The contemporaneous American Draft provides indication of a greater concern for the rights of the accused and thus a better foundation for ultimate legitimacy. Specifically, that draft contains provisions that ensure: "[r]easonable notice . . . of the charges . . . and of the opportunity to defend;"[82] the receipt of all charging and related documents;[83] a "fair opportunity to be heard . . . and to have the assistance of counsel;"[84] a right to 'full particulars;"[85] the open presentation of evidence;[86] and complete discovery of any written matter "to be introduced."[87]

The final procedures adopted by the parties in the IMT Charter reflect a greater concern for the procedural protections of the accused. The IMT Charter provided the accused with all of the rights proposed in the American Draft presented at the close of the International Conference on Military Trials held during the summer of 1945.[88] Further, these rights were expanded to include: translation of the trial into a language that was understood by the accused;[89] a clear right to "present evidence . . . in the support of his defense;"[90] and the right

---

[82] Last Draft of American Annex, Paragraph 14(a) (1945), *reprinted at* INTERNATIONAL CONFERENCE REPORT, *supra* note 56, at 167, 179.

[83] *Id.* para. 14(b), at 179.

[84] *Id.*

[85] *Id.* para. 11.

[86] *Id.*

[87] *Id.*

[88] *Compare generally* IMT CHARTER art. 16 *with* American Draft, *supra* notes 82-87 and accompanying text.

[89] IMT CHARTER, *supra* note 14, art. 16(c).

[90] *Id.* art. 16(e).

to "cross examine any witness called by the prosecution."[91] The accused, however, did not

enjoy the right against self-incrimination and the Tribunal retained the power to "interrogate

any defendant."[92]

The procedures developed to protect the rights of the accused major war criminals agreed

upon by the principle Allies demonstrated a remarkable movement from the early notions of

Winston Churchill.[93] In their final state the procedures of the IMT were well planned to meet

the needs of justice. Though confrontation of witnesses was guaranteed to the defense, the

judges at the IMT were given great latitude in determining the admissibility of sworn and

unsworn documents and to accept evidence that under British and American law would have

been found to violate the rule against hearsay.[94] The Tribunal was also given authority to

take judicial notice of a wide class of documents including those prepared by Allied nations

in preparation of and resulting from other national tribunals conducted by any of the

members of the IMT.[95]

---

[91] *Id.*

[92] *Id.* art. 17(b).

[93] *See supra* note 29 and accompanying text.

[94] *See* IMT CHARTER, *supra* note 14, art. 19. Article 19 provides that the "Tribunal shall not be bound by technical rules of evidence . . . and shall admit any evidence which it deems to have probative value."

[95] This article permits the judicial notice of a broad class of documentary material. Specifically, of "official governmental documents and reports of the United Nations, including the acts and documents of the committees set up in the various Allied countries for the investigation of war crimes, and the records and findings of military or other tribunals of any of the United Nations." *Id.* art. 21.

When closely examined, these procedures read in conjunction with the power to establish a "Committee for the Investigation and Prosecution of Major War Criminals"[96] could have been utilized to permit the prosecutor to prepare a "paper case" followed by the presentation of any evidence by the defense. This, however, did not occur. And though the IMT relied heavily on the benefits of relaxed evidentiary rules, it did hear some testimony in support of all the indictments presented.

The procedures adopted served the IMT and the international community well in meeting the goal of legitimizing the verdicts handed down at Nuremberg. Although the procedures permitted a relaxed evidentiary norm, the Tribunal was composed of seasoned jurists from several well developed legal systems. Further, the facts developed by the documents deemed admissible pursuant to the relaxed rules appear to have been well established and corroborated in the record. Accordingly, the arguments of the defense often rested more on the legal theory upon which culpability was based rather than a dispute of the underlying facts alleged.[97]

4. Perceived Fairness of the IMT at Nuremberg

---

[96] This committee was established under the provisions of the IMT Charter articles 14 and 15.

[97] This was a common occurrence both the two international military tribunals and the national commissions conducted in both the Pacific and Germany. *See infra* notes 222-224 and accompanying test.

Modern writers often view tribunals such as the IMT as courts of "victor's justice."[98] Scholars and lawyers of the day often had a different view of the IMT. Notably, German scholars and lawyers often commented on the extent to which the IMT went to ensure impartiality. One contemporary German legal scholar noted that "[n]obody dares to doubt that [the IMT] was guided by the search for truth and justice from the first to the last day of this tremendous trial."[99] Further, even the defense counsel for Alfred Jodl noted that while critical of what he perceived to be the *ex post facto* nature of the proceedings, that his interactions with the Secretary General of the Tribunal had been "chivalrous" and had been of great assistance in providing "documents of a decisive nature and very important literature." He further noted that such assistance would not have been otherwise possible before a domestic court in post-war Germany in light of the degraded conditions of government institutions.[100] Ironically, much of the greatest criticism of the IMT came from within the profession of arms of a variety of nations. [101] But criticism also flowed from many jurists, lawyers and politicians in the United States.

The esteemed jurist Judge Learned Hand regarded the prosecutions as "a step backward in international law" and "a precedent that will prove embarrassing, if not disastrous, in the

---

[98] *See, e.g.*, David L. Herman, *A Dish Best Not Served at All: How Foreign Military War Crimes Suspects Lack Protections Under United States and International Law*, 172 MIL. L. REV. 40 (2002) (author critical of "victor's justice" tribunals and focuses upon weakness in trials such as that of Japanese General Masaharu Homma).

[99] Ra. Th. Klefisch, *Thoughts About Purport and Effect of the Nuremberg Judgment*, 2 JURISTISCHE RUNDSCHAU 45 (1947), *reprinted in* NUREMBERG: GERMAN VIEWS OF THE WAR TRIALS 201, 201 (Wilbourne E. Benton, ed. 1955) (translated by Georg Grimm).

[100] Statement of Dr. Hermann Jahrreiss, XVII Trial of the Major War Criminals Before the International Military Tribunal 458-94 (Nuremberg 1948).

[101] DOENITZ AT NUREMBERG: A REAPPRAISAL – WAR CRIMES AND THE MILITARY PROFESSIONAL (H.K. Thompson, Jr., et al. eds., 1976).

future."[102] Major General Ulysses S Grant III echoed many of the concerns of military officers on both sides of the conflict. General Grant noted that in his opinion the "trial of officers and even civilian officials was a most unfortunate . . . violation of international law . . . . it [gives] a precedent for the victor to revenge itself on individuals after any future war."[103]

These criticisms appear to have flowed from a blend of concern over the potential for criminal responsibility *ex post facto*, and a fear that future military leaders could be held accountable for their actions when they were following orders. General Matthew Ridgway commented that prosecutions of those in uniform who acted "under the orders or directives of their superiors . . . is unjustified and repugnant to the code of enlightened governments."[104]

But the concern that these trials were based upon conduct criminalized *ex post facto* was not universally held. The IMT proponents and jurists rejected these concerns noting that the major war criminals were on notice of what was considered to be unlawful acts in war and against peace.[105] Further, scholars from Germany writing during the late 1940s note that the German people after the collapse of the Third Reich supported the results of the Trials at Nuremberg. In the words of one German scholar:

---

[102] *Id.* at 1.

[103] *Id.* at 9.

[104] *Id.* at 181.

[105] *See supra* notes 34-38 and accompanying text.

the entire German population feels [the Nuremberg offenses] merit the death penalty. These crimes would also have found their retribution by applying the penal codes in force in most nations, including Germany. It is also the conviction of the German people that the society of nations, if it wishes to survive . . . may and must secure itself against such crimes also with the weapons of law.[106]

As with the German population, the American public overwhelmingly supported the Tribunals as a means to bring closure to the war in Europe. This support was broadly held in the journalistic and academic community as well as with the general public. Overall public support for the Tribunals at their conclusion was at seventy-five percent with nearly seventy percent of columnists, seventy-three percent of newspapers and seventy-five percent of the scholarly periodicals reflecting a positive view of the process and the Judgment.[107]

5. Role of Court as Part of Larger Reconstruction Plan.

The Allies began to develop plans on how to punish German war criminals before the end of World War II. Disagreement existed as to whether the most serious violators of the law of war should be tried at all. Prime Minister Winston Churchill argued unsuccessfully that so-called "arch-criminals" should be summarily executed upon identification.[108] Some within

---

[106] Hans Ehard, *The Nuremberg Trial Against the Major War Criminals and International Law*, 3 SUDDEUTSCHE JURISTEN-ZEITUNG 353 (1948), *reprinted in* NUREMBERG: GERMAN VIEWS OF THE WAR TRIALS 76, 78 (Wilbourne E. Benton, ed., 1955) (translation by E.C. Jann).

[107] MICHAEL R. MARRUS, THE NUREMBERG WAR CRIMES TRIAL 1945-46: A DOCUMENTARY HISTORY 243 (1997).

[108] TELFORD TAYLOR, THE ANATOMY OF THE NUREMBERG TRIALS 34 (1992).

the United States War Department supported a "guilt by association" theory that provided proof of membership in organizations such as the Nazi party alone would establish guilt.[109]

The framers of the IMT Charter were concerned that the Tribunal maintain legitimacy in the eyes of the German population and that it contribute to the overall restoration of the rule of law.[110] By rejecting expedient theories of responsibility such as a "Nazi party membership" standard of culpability, the Allies successfully made the IMT an instrument of positive reconstruction as opposed to a court of vengeance.[111] In the end, the interests of justice were met and punishment meted out to those found deserving. As important, the court served to compliment the overall return of civil society to Germany rather than serve solely as a quasi-judicial extension of war.

The IMT's emphasis on procedural protections for the accused, transparency in practice, and its demonstrated desire to act in accordance with the rule of law helped to "jump-start" the German civil society in the wake of a devastating war. Although a martial court by its

---

[109] *Id. at* 36. Under this approach, it was proposed that punishment would then be based upon the extent to which one participated in the Party or had knowledge of its activities. *Id.*

[110] Brigadier General Telford Taylor felt the activities at Nuremberg and before the various commissions were critical to the reintroduction of the German people to democracy. For this reason, he recommended that the proceedings of the various forums be published and widely distributed. One of the three stated reasons of "leading importance" to this endeavor was "To promote the interest of historical truth and to aid in the reestablishment of democracy in Germany." TELFORD TAYLOR, FINAL REPORT TO THE SECREATARY OF THE ARMY ON THE NUERNBERG WAR CRIMES TRIALS UNDER CONTROL COUNCIL LAW NO. 10, 101 (1949).

[111] There was, however, some prosecutions based upon membership in organizations coupled with other subsequent crimes. There were no convictions based solely upon membership before the IMT, but there were some convictions based upon memberships in various organs of the Nazi establishment where the accused was acquitted of the other substantive crimes. Thus, the "membership" crime was a stocking stuffer charge added to the other crimes charged. Those who were simply found to be members of organizations found criminal were processed through an administrative procedure called Spruchkammern which was conducted outside of Control Law No. 10 and was a component of the German de-Nazification program. *Id.* at 16-17.

nature, it set the stage for the return of the civil courts by emphasizing the need for a methodical search for justice consistent with the rule of law. Its work helped to set a professional standard for the post-war German judiciary.

Further, the IMT, along with other military commissions, served as part of the bridge from war to peace. The adherence to procedural requirements and the rule of law furthered the ends of reconciliation. The alternative – expedient process – would have furthered existing divides. The IMT was a key cornerstone in the development of a lasting peace and the future friendship between Germany and her former foes. [112]

6. Were the stated goals accomplished?

If the *efficient* administration of post conflict justice was the sole standard by which to judge the IMT it would be deemed a failure. The process was lengthy, cumbersome in its multilateral development[113] and was a source of frustration for its contemporary architects.[114] Though the writings of the day demonstrate that while efficiency was of concern to the

---

[112] Scholars have argued that the process of German introspection brought about by the trials of war criminals played an important role in setting the stage for the successful implementation of the Marshall Plan and the subsequent transformation of Germany into an American ally. Wendy Toon, *Genocide on Trial*, (2001) (book review) *available at* http://www.ihrinfo.ac.uk/reviews/paper/toonW.html.

[113] This process required close negotiations with the Soviet Union which could prove difficult because of language and cultural differences. With work these differences were successfully overcome. *See* FRANCIS BIDDLE, IN BRIEF AUTHORITY 427-28 (Doubleday 1962), relevant excerpts *reprinted at* MICHAEL R. MARRUS, THE NUREMBERG WAR CRIMES TRIAL 1945-46: A DOCUMENTARY HISTORY 246-48 (1997).

[114] For a good discussion of the initial difficulties of getting the major Allied parties on board for a single judicial solution, *see* WILLIAM J. BOSCH, JUDGMENT ON NUREMBERG 26-27 (1970). Bosch discusses the range of approaches considered from "catch-identify-shoot," *id.* at 24, to "drumhead court-martials without any involved legal procedures" (SIC), *id*, to a "program of international trials." *Id.* at 26.

planners, it was secondary to the need to establish the legitimacy of the court and to provide a method of accountability that served to further the restoration of peace and reconciliation.

From this standard, the IMT was a success. The IMT was not a system of post conflict justice that was conducted alongside the reconstruction of Germany – it was a fundamental process in the restoration of peace in Germany. Though other methods of justice may have served the needs of punishment of the wrongdoer in a more efficient manner, many would have failed to complement the overall reconstruction efforts or may have been overly detrimental to the ultimate goal of reconciliation of the belligerencies. While Winston Churchill's summary execution proposal would have been efficient, it would have set a poor standard for the future and damaged the fragile relationship that existed between the victor and the vanquished.[115] Other methods, such as secret procedures, or sole reliance on national military commissions would have lacked the signs of international cooperation that helped provide a thin layer of legitimacy to an otherwise novel approach to the trial of international war criminals.

The ultimate sign of success has come with the passage of time. Though modern writers are split on issues related to the fairness of the procedures and the overall efficiency of the process, there can be no debate that the reconstruction of Germany after World War II

---

[115] The German people of the day were becoming increasingly acquainted with the brutality of our World War II ally, and their ally in their invasion of Poland, the Soviet Union. Although the Soviet Union participated in the IMT, the broader roles taken on by the United States in their zone of occupation and that of the Soviet Union marked a stark contrast even before the construction of the Berlin wall. Though perhaps impossible to quantify, there can be little doubt that the stark contrast in approach that the United States and Britain took toward a conquered Germany played a significant role in keeping the German people predominately behind the west during the cold war with the Soviet Union.

established the foundation for the longest period of peace in the history of modern Europe.[116] The IMT was key to the formulation of this success.

The IMT met its goals in a difficult environment and was successful in both the short and long term in its contribution to a lasting peace. The establishment of the IMT also helped to forge the way for the creation of a similar tribunal in East Asia. Though many of the issues facing that Tribunal were similar to those faced by the IMT, the Tokyo tribunal also faced an exceedingly difficult cultural environment. While it was necessary for the IMT to establish its legitimacy among the German population, its ability to establish its legitimacy was enhanced by many common cultural attributes among the victors and the vanquished. The Tribunal sitting at Tokyo, however, had to establish its legitimacy within a governmental and legal order alien to western conceptions of justice. Because of this key distinction, the IMTFE yields very valuable lessons for today.

B. IMTFE [117]

---

[116] *See, e.g.,* Wendy Toon, *Genocide on Trial,* (2001) (book review) *available at* http://www.ihrinfo.ac.uk/reviews/paper/toonW.html.

[117] The primary source material for the Tokyo Trials can be found in the Transcript of the International Japanese War Crimes Trial which comprises 209 volumes of text plus exhibits. The Judge Advocate General's School, Army in Charlottesville, Virginia has a complete set. The Transcripts, however, are intimidating and very difficult to navigate. When undertaking research into the area, it would be advisable to locate a library with THE TOKYO MAJOR WAR CRIMES TRIAL: THE RECORDS OF THE INTERNATIONAL MILITARY TRIBUNAL FOR THE FAR EAST (R. John Pritchard, ed., 1998) , or, in the alternative, his earlier work THE TOKYO WAR CRIMES TRIAL: THE COMPLETE TRANSCRIPTS OF THE PROCEEDINGS OF THE INTERNATIONAL MILITARY TRIBUNAL FOR THE FAR EAST (R. John Pritchard, ed., Garland 1981). The 1998 citation with its excellent annotation is a great resource for gaining access to the wealth of information contained in the Transcripts of the IMTFE. Citations to the transcripts contained herein are to the primary source, however.

[F]or a catalogue of depravity and wholesale violations of the law of war, one really should examine the Tokyo Trials.[118]

1. Stated Goals of the IMTFE

As with the International Military Tribunal in Nuremberg, the International Military Tribunal for the Far East (IMTFE) was one part of an overall program to reintegrate the conquered into civil society. Unlike Germany, however, Japan had never developed many of the legal traditions found in other Axis countries before the outbreak of war. Lawyers were low level functionaries in a legal hierarchy with little concern for individual liberties or civil rights.[119] A key objective of American foreign policy after the surrender of Japan was to develop a respect for the rule of law and human rights among the citizens of Japan. The pacification of Japan was to include a complete disarmament[120] and policies to encourage "a desire for individual liberties and respect for fundamental human rights."[121]

Further, the scope of the IMTFE was broader than the IMT in that it had jurisdiction over atrocities committed during three distinct phases of Japanese aggression: the Manchurian Incident (1931); the "China Incident of 1937-1945"; and Japanese operations in the Pacific

---

[118] H. Wayne Elliott, *The Nuremberg War Crimes Trials CD-Rom*, 149 MIL. L. REV. 312, 316 (1995).

[119] I POLITICAL REORIENTATION OF JAPAN 190 (1949).

[120] United States Initial Post-Surrender Policy for Japan, August 29, 1945, DEP'T ST. PUB. 267, OCCUPATION OF JAPAN – POLICY AND PROGRESS, 1946, at 73, 74 [hereinafter Japan Policy].

[121] *Id.*

during World War II.[122] Further, unlike the IMT, the hearings spanned years not months, and was a major consumer of post-war funds and resources. At its peak, the IMTFE employed approximately 230 translators, 237 lawyers, and consumed nearly twenty-five percent of all of the paper used by the Allies during the occupation of Japan.[123] This unprecedented dedication of resources to post-conflict justice demonstrates the degree of importance that the Supreme Commander and the governments of the respective Allies placed on this aspect of societal reconstruction.

After the surrender of Japan, General of the Army Douglas MacArthur was designated as the Supreme Commander for the Allied Powers and on September 6, 1945 very broad powers were delegated to him by the civilian leadership of the United States. His powers were clear – he was to be the head of the Japanese state during its occupation with "[t]he authority of the Emperor and the Japanese Government to rule the State [ ] subordinate to you as Supreme Commander for the Allied Powers."[124] Notwithstanding this great delegation of authority, there was also a profound concern for the immediate normalization of domestic governance within this new social paradigm imposed upon Japan. The architects of post war Japan made it clear that General MacArthur was in law and fact the Supreme Commander, but they also

---

[122] 2 THE TOKYO MAJOR WAR CRIMES TRIAL: THE RECORDS OF THE INTERNATIONAL MILITARY TRIBUNAL FOR THE FAR EAST xxiv (R. John Pritchard, ed., 1998).

[123] *Id.* at xxv.

[124] Authority of General MacArthur as Supreme Commander for the Allied Powers, Sept. 6, 1945, *reprinted in* DEP'T ST. PUB. 267, OCCUPATION OF JAPAN – POLICY AND PROGRESS 88-9 (1946).

directed that "[c]ontrol of Japan shall be exercised through the Japanese Government to the extent that such an arrangement produces satisfactory results."[125]

From the beginning of the occupation of Japan, Japanese officials and citizens were integrated into the operation of the Japanese occupation which could be called the Japanese experiment. Although many of the procedures and goals for Japan reflected those being developed as part of Europe's reconstruction, the challenges that faced General MacArthur eclipsed those faced in the European theater.[126] Specifically, Germany was forced to be reintroduced to the rule of law, democracy and respect for individual rights. Germany was brought back onto a long path leading to the creation of modern liberal democracies that can be traced back to pre-Socratic thought. For Japan, the path to liberal democracy began with the sound of atomic thunderclaps followed by the arrival of General Douglas MacArthur.

Key to the success of this experiment was the exposure of the Japanese population to the rule of law as exercised by regularly organized tribunals bound by rules of procedure and burdens of proof. Though the horrors that the Japanese visited upon uniformed prisoners of war eclipse those perpetrated by other Axis powers both in scope and savagery, Japanese soldiers would nonetheless be given procedural protections similar to those of the IMT. Contrary to the summary executions initially envision by Winston Churchill for major

---

[125] *Id.*

[126] *See supra* notes 40-49 and accompanying text.

34

German war criminals,[127] they were to be given their day in court before the IMTFE as well as other national military commissions.

The willingness of the victors to adopt such procedures with an enemy that routinely tortured, maimed[128] and even ate their prisoners of war[129] stood in stark contrast with the execution of executive authority previously known to Japanese imperial subjects.[130] This willingness to substitute a legal process for passionate vengeance served to bring the actions of the Supreme Commander in conformity with the new society in which the United States and her Allies wished to create in Japan. General Douglas MacArthur saw his mission as no

---

[127] *See supra* note 29.

[128] The techniques used by the Japanese to impose POW camp discipline seemed to only be limited by the creativity of their captures. Techniques included: "exposing the victim to the hot tropical sun for long hours without headdress or other protection; suspension of the victim by his arms in such a manner as at times to force the arms from their sockets; binding the victim where he would be attacked by insects . . . . [or] forced to run in a circle without shoes over broken glass while being spurred on by Japanese soldiers who beat them with rifle buts." United States and 10 Other Nations v. Araki and 27 Other Defendants, 203 Trans. Int'l Jap. War Cr. Trial 49,702-03 (1948) (extract from Tribunal's Judgment). The Tribunal went on to find that the Japanese routinely included mass execution as collective punishment often executing members from the same prisoner group as any POW that successfully escaped. *Id.* at 49,702-04.

[129] A challenge for post war prosecutors of the day was to find prosecutorial theories that could be utilized to prosecute savagery of the nature that the Japanese inflicted upon others. The Australians included within their definition of "war crimes" two acts particularly unique to the Japanese in the modern history of war: cannibalism and "mutilation of a dead body." These crimes then were charged in the initial salvo of Australian military commissions. R. PICCIGALLO, THE JAPANESE ON TRIAL: ALLIED WAR CRIMES OPERATIONS IN THE EAST 128-29 (1979).

[130] The Japanese subjects were not exposed to notions of liberal democracy and experienced life in a totalitarian regime where "rights and dignity of the individual, and economic freedom . . . [had] never before been known." BRIGADIER GENERAL COURTNEY WHITNEY, *The Philosophy of Occupation, reprinted in* I POLITICAL REORIENTATION OF JAPAN xvii, xx (1949).

less than the establishment "upon Japanese soil a bastion to the democratic concept."[131] The use of summary procedures would have been antithetical to this unprecedented objective.

Though antithetical to the mission of the Allies, summary procedures and show trials were not alien to the Japanese criminal justice system in the years leading up to World War II. Japanese criminal defendants were provided hearings, but rather than providing the accused with due process of law, these trials served more to ratify confessions obtained by police investigators. In other cases, especially with "thought criminals," trials were replaced by brutal summary executions.[132] When trial was necessary, however, police often would resort to cruel methods of torture to ensure confessions. These methods included inserting needles under the fingernails of suspects,[133] crushing fingers,[134] beating thighs and piercing

---

[131] GENERAL OF THE ARMY DOUGLAS H. MACARTHUR, *Three Years*, *in* I POLITICAL REORIENTATION OF JAPAN v, v (1949). The words and philosophy of General MacArthur ring true today as the United States faces malignant regimes whose populations have significant underlying cultural differences than those known in modern western democracies. General MacArthur saw the creation of a democratic "bastion" in Japan as a substantive retort to the "fallacy of the oft-expressed dogma that the East and the West are separated by such impenetrable social, cultural and racial distinctions as to render impossible the absorption by the one of the ideas and concepts of the other." *Id.* at vi. Those considering the fate of failed and failing states should evaluate the reconstruction of Japan and its success before rejecting similar efforts solely on the basis of impossibility. A minority of academic scholars of the Middle East argues that the United States should ignore the naysayers and impose modern reforms in Iraq, unilaterally if necessary. For an excellent discussion of this provocative and unapologetic approach to Iraq, *see* Fouad Ajami, *Iraq and the Arab's Future*, 82 FOR. AFF. 2 (2003). Professor Ajami, of Johns Hopkins University's School for Advanced International Studies, makes the point directly that Japan is the precedent for post-Saddam Hussein Iraq. Ajami argues "the Japanese precedent is an important one . . . . It was victor's justice that drove the new monumental undertaking and powered the twin goals of demilitarization and democratization. The victors tinkered with the media, the educational system, and the textbooks. Those are some of the things that will have to be done if a military campaign in Iraq is to redeem itself in the process." *Id.* at 15.

[132] One particular set of brutal summary executions occurred when a group of 10 pro-labor radicals were jailed for singing "illegal revolutionary songs" from the top of the labor building. When the men refused to stop making noise once jailed, a local military group was brought in to resolve the matter expediently. Their expedient action involved killing them by burning and decapitation. RICHARD H. MITCHELL, JANUS-FACED JUSTICE: POLITICAL CRIMINALS IN IMPERIAL JAPAN 41 (1992).

[133] *Id.* at 55.

[134] *Id.*

eardrums to name a few.[135] Torture of female communists appeared to be at the hands of sexual sadists.[136] Such extreme measures were accepted by the government as in the words of a police training book of 1930s Japan, "[u]nlike a murderer, who kills only one or perhaps several people, and there it ends, thought criminals endanger the life of the entire nation."[137]

It is from this legal environment upon which the IMTFE was to be superimposed. It is also against this backdrop that one must consider modern criticism of the Tribunal itself.[138] It is not possible to evaluate the effectiveness of the IMTFE without considering the legal landscape upon which it was grafted.

Thus, the importance of the process set into motion by the Allies can not be understated as it served to harmonize several competing goals for the reorganization and "political reorientation of Japan."[139] This process ensured the trial of the wrongdoer[140] before a regularly constituted tribunal. This process was steeped more in reason than passion and

---

[135] *Id.*

[136] *Id.* at 82.

[137] *Id.* at 88 (citation omitted).

[138] *See infra* notes 173-180 and accompanying text.

[139] There is no phrase that better captures what the United States sought to accomplish in Japan. It has been lifted wholesale from 1 POLITICAL REORIENTATION OF JAPAN i (1949).

[140] This goal is common to any criminal court and also serves other traditional goals of the justice system to include retribution and deterrence. As will be discussed, *infra*, it is the opinion of the author that too much emphasis is placed upon these basic goals of a domestic justice system when seeking to develop and implement systems of international prospective criminal justice as with the International Criminal Court. *See infra* notes 306-307 and accompanying text.

helped to further the reconciliation of the belligerents.[141] It also served as a crucial

introduction to the role of courts as an instrument of accountability bound to respect the

rights to procedural process of even the most vile accused.[142] Further, public trials in which

publicity was not only authorized but encouraged ensured that the Japanese civilian

population became aware of the atrocities that had been committed by their government

officials and soldiers.[143]

2. Charter & Duration

As with the Charter of the IMT,[144] the Charter of the IMTFE served to limit its

jurisdiction to only "major war criminals."[145] This limited scope of jurisdiction ensured that

the Tribunal would be able to meet the needs of Justice without being bogged down in the

---

[141] Although at least one leader of an Allied power, Winston Churchill, believed that summary execution was legal and appropriate with serious violators of the law of war, this method of justice was not utilized in Japan. *See supra* note 29. The creation of a court to hold individuals accountable for their wrongdoing served to vent the vengeance of populations such as those in the United States and Australia who had their family members victimized brutally by the Japanese. It also served to reduce the level of passion and belligerency between the parties to the hostilities by holding open courts in which the evidence was presented and the defense were given an opportunity to present a case with the assistance of counsel. Rather than setting the stage for another round of violence, the method in which the trials were conducted served the interests of justice while serving to legitimize the actions of the victors in the eyes of the domestic Japanese population thus helping to meet the goal of reconciliation.

[142] This aspect of the IMTFE provided a cornerstone to the political reorientation of Japan that in less than a generation resulted in the complete transformation of a medieval society characterized by unquestioned, hereditary executive authority, militarism and disregard for basic human rights into a modern liberal democracy.

[143] PHILIP R. PICCIGALLO, THE JAPANESE ON TRIAL: ALLIED WAR CRIMES OPERATIONS IN THE EAST 15 (1979).

[144] *See supra* notes 50-58 and accompanying text.

[145] Charter of the International Military Tribunal for the Far East art. 1 (January 19, 1946), *reprinted in* DEP'T ST. PUB. 267, OCCUPATION OF JAPAN – POLICY AND PROGRESS, 1946, at 147, 149 [hereinafter IMTFE Charter].

prosecution of second tier criminals. It also provided some protection from claims that the Tribunal was exercising its jurisdiction in an inconsistent manner.

Further, the IMTFE's limited jurisdiction over "major" war criminals was complimented by the clear intent of the Supreme Commander that other "international, national or occupation court[s or] commissions" would also be operating within the Far Eastern theater.[146] This complimentary judicial regime served to maximize the reach of the justice system by creating lesser courts that could focus on lower level criminals. It also served to provide forums for individual nations to prosecute war criminals of particular interest such as those that may have tortured their prisoners of war.

The IMTFE Charter is silent as to its intended duration except for a statement that its "permanent" seat was to be in Tokyo.[147] Unlike the IMT, however, it is not as clear that the IMTFE was to end its work after its first series of prosecutions as was the case in Germany.[148] Though in practice it followed the same path as the IMT, it is not as clear that the drafters and participants were as confident that domestic courts in Japan could handle such cases if it became necessary at a later date.

3. Tribunal Composition & Procedure

---

[146] Establishment of an International Military Tribunal for the Far East, SCAP Special Proclamation (January 19, 1946), *in* DEP'T ST. PUB. 267, OCCUPATION OF JAPAN – POLICY AND PROGRESS, 1946, at 31, 32.

[147] IMTFE CHARTER, *supra* note 145, art. 1.

[148] *See supra* note 58 and accompanying text.

The IMTFE built upon the same sources of law that formed the foundation of the IMT. The IMTFE, however, also cited the creation and use of international tribunals at Nuremberg as precedent.[149] But the composition of the IMTFE was much broader than its cousin in Europe. The IMTFE brought together representatives from a collection of the victors, the formerly vanquished and the tortured.

a. Tribunal Composition

The Supreme Allied Commander selected the tribunal's membership from a list of nominations presented by the signatories of the Instrument of Surrender with Japan along with nominations from India and the Philippines.[150] The Supreme Commander could convene a Tribunal consisting of between six and eleven members selected from the nominees presented.[151] Further, the Supreme Commander had the power to designate the President of the Tribunal.[152] The President had the power not only to resolve evenly divided disputes as to matters of procedure and evidence, but also to break any tie concerning guilt or

---

[149] DEP'T ST. PUB. 267, OCCUPATION OF JAPAN – POLICY AND PROGRESS 28-29 (1946).

[150] IMTFE CHARTER, *supra* note 145, art. 2. The parties to the Instrument of Surrender were the United States, the Republic of China, the United Kingdom, Australia, the USSR, Canada, France, the Netherlands, and New Zealand. *See* Instrument of Surrender, September 2, 1945, Allied Powers – Japan.

[151] *Id.*

[152] *Id.* art. 3(a).

innocence.[153] General MacArthur appointed an Australian, Sir William Webb, to serve in this important position.[154]

Unlike the IMT, the IMTFE did not require the continuous representation of all countries at the Tribunal to constitute a quorum.[155] Six members were required for a quorum and absence did not disqualify a member from further service on the case so long as he did not disqualify himself "by reason of insufficient familiarity with the proceedings which took place in the case."[156] Such absence, however, had less impact upon a tribunal member than might normally be suspected. Specifically, the difficulties in translation among the various witnesses often made it necessary for tribunal members to review translated transcripts after the fact along with volumes of other documentary evidence.[157]

b. Tribunal Procedure

The jurisdiction of the IMTFE was limited to three classes of criminalized activity. "Crimes against Peace,"[158] "Conventional War Crimes,"[159] and "Crimes against

---

[153] *Id.* art. 4(b).

[154] PHILIP R. PICCIGALLO, THE JAPANESE ON TRIAL: ALLIED WAR CRIMES OPERATIONS IN THE EAST 11 (1979).

[155] IMTFE CHARTER, *supra* note 145, art. 4(a).

[156] *Id.* art. 4(c).

[157] PHILIP R. PICCIGALLO, THE JAPANESE ON TRIAL: ALLIED WAR CRIMES OPERATIONS IN THE EAST 18 (1979).

[158] Crimes against peace were defined as those involving the "planning, preparation, initiation or waging of a declared, or undeclared war of aggression, or a war in violation of international law, [or agreement]." IMTFE CHARTER, *supra* note 145, art. 5(a).

Humanity."[160] Personal jurisdiction was limited to "major war criminals"[161] and the court maintained concurrent jurisdiction along with any other "international, national or occupation court . . . ."[162] Notwithstanding the concurrent jurisdiction of national courts, the overall policy of the Allies was coordinated and refined by the Far Eastern Commission (FEC).[163] In April 1946, the FEC promulgated a "Policy Decision" coordinating and authorizing the trials of war criminals before national courts in conjunction with the IMTFE.

The determination of which defendants would stand trial before the IMTFE was placed in the hands of the International Prosecution Staff (IPS).[164] The IPS, composed of prosecutors from all of the countries represented in the FEC, was also responsible for preparing the indictment against the accused. Each indictment lodged with the IMTFE by the Chief Prosecutor reflected a blend of the approaches of "eleven legal systems" with ultimate concurrence from each member nation's representative on the IPS.[165] This process further served to legitimize the work of the IMTFE as only upon a broad concurrence of prosecutors

---

[159] "War crimes" were simply defined as "violations of the laws or customs of war." *Id.* art. 5(b).

[160] "Crimes against humanity" focused on atrocities committed against civilian populations to include "murder, extermination, enslavement, deportation, and other inhumane acts" to include "persecutions on political or racial grounds." *Id.* art. 5(c).

[161] *Id.* art. 1.

[162] Establishment of an International Military Tribunal for the Far East, SCAP Special Proclamation (January 19, 1946), *in* DEP'T ST. PUB. 267, OCCUPATION OF JAPAN – POLICY AND PROGRESS, 1946, at 31, 32. [hereinafter Proclamation].

[163] PHILIP R. PICCIGALLO, THE JAPANESE ON TRIAL: ALLIED WAR CRIMES OPERATIONS IN THE EAST 34 (1979).

[164] *Id.* at 13.

[165] *Id.* at 14 (citation omitted).

from numerous backgrounds as to the status of the evidence and the theory of criminality could a prosecution progress.

Once subject to indictment before the IMTFE, Japanese accused were provided a wide variety of procedural protections consistent with those available to western common law jurisdictions. These protections ensured: the accused would be made aware of the charges against him in an "indictment . . . consist[ing] of a plain, concise, and adequate statement of each offense charged;"[166] "adequate time for defense;"[167] to have access to translated proceedings and documents as "needed and requested;"[168] the right to be represented by counsel of his own request;[169] the right to reasonable examination of any witness;[170] and broad authority to request the production of witnesses and documentation.[171] These protections were embraced by the Tribunal and great efforts were undertaken to ensure that the accused were given access to superior counsel and any favorable evidence that they might reasonably desire.[172]

---

[166] IMTFE CHARTER, *supra* note 145, art. 9(a).

[167] *Id.* art. 9(a).

[168] *Id.* art. 9(b).

[169] *Id.* art. 9(c). The tribunal could disapprove the request for the individually requested counsel, and also was required to appoint an attorney to represent the accused if requested. Further, the court had the right to appoint counsel for an unrepresented accused *ab initio* "if necessary to provide for a fair trial." *Id.*

[170] *Id.* art. 9(e).

[171] *Id.*

[172] This right was provided in the language of the IMTFE Charter itself. The Charter provided that the defense could request in writing the "production of witnesses or of documents." This request was to state where the requested person or material was thought to be and state the relevancy of the material requested. *Id.*

4. *Perceived Fairness of the IMTFE*

Scholars vary in opinion as to whether the IMTFE provided a fair forum for those in the dock. Those critical of the proceedings cite weak due process protections, vague or non-existent bases for non-retrospective criminality,[173] and even disingenuous motivations on the part of the Allies to legitimize their war against and destruction of Japan while using a court to "barely disguise[] revenge."[174] These criticisms echo those leveled by critics of the IMT.

One sobering criticism is of the IMTFE stems from the lack of any direct evidence of official orders to commit mass atrocities. Though there is ample circumstantial evidence that the supreme leadership either should have known, or did in fact know, of the atrocities carried out in the field by their subordinates, no evidence existed that they directed atrocities.[175] In fact, the Tribunal in its Judgment conceded this point by noting that with

---

[173] Crimes against the peace is the category that is most troublesome to many concerned about criminal law being applied *ex post facto*. *See* Onuma Yasuaki, *The Tokyo Trial: Between Law and Politics*, *in* THE TOKYO WAR CRIMES TRIAL: AN INTERNATIONAL SYMPOSIUM 45 (C. Hosoya, N. Ando, Y. Onuma, R. Minear, eds., 1986). Yasuaki also criticizes the inability of the IMTFE to take jurisdiction over what he considers to be Allied atrocities such as the use of atomic weapons and the violation of the Neutrality Pact by the USSR. *Id.* Another criticism of Yasuaki that might be of greater merit is the failure to consider more representation on the IMTFE from countries that bore the immediate thrust of Japan's violence, such as Korea and Malaysia. *Id.* at 46. As discussed herein at *infra* notes 350-354 and accompanying text, future post-conflict tribunals should consider such broad representation.

[174] RICHARD H. MINEAR, VICTORS' JUSTICE: THE TOKYO WAR CRIMES TRIAL 19 (1971). This author is somewhat bemusing and he does not like others having the post-conflict justice cake after Tokyo, but he, himself likes the cake, appears to want the cake, and will eat it too. Notwithstanding his critique that Tokyo was "disguised revenge," he notes in other areas of his book the certain need to try folks such as Lieutenant Calley as "essential to American honor" with no mention of justice and more than a tinge of revenge. Further, he goes on to elaborate and intimate that he "favors strongly" prosecuting "at least two American presidents" for their role in committing war crimes in Viet Nam. As with so many of the moral relativists that spring from the "Viet Nam Genre" of scholars, their arguments against one matter are often undercut by their desire to do the same in another context. It appears as to the "fairness" of a concept to this author of the cited work is somewhat dependant upon whether Tojo or Richard Nixon is sitting in the dock.

[175] I THE TOKYO JUDGMENT xv (B. V. A. Roling & C. F. Ruter, eds., 1977).

respect to the mass commission of conventional war crimes, that they must have either been "secretly ordered or willfully permitted by the Japanese Government or individual members thereof and by the leaders of the armed forces."[176] Such critics note that former Japanese Prime Minister Hirota Koki was sentenced to death for failing proactively to prevent the Rape of Nanking though there was a significant question as to whether his position gave him any real power to do so.[177]

Further, some commentators commented that the quality of the jurists selected for service both as judges and prosecutors were substandard, especially when compared to those tapped for similar service before the IMT. The President of the IMTFE, Australian Sir William Webb, has been described by one former member of the Tribunal, B.V.A. Roling, as "unsure of his power" and "dictatorial" in his relations with both his colleagues on the bench and the counsel before him.[178] This stands in stark contrast with the perception of the English Presiding Judge at Nuremberg, Sir Geoffrey Lawrence, who came "to personify Justice" even in the eyes of the defendants.[179] Though Roling seeks to identify such contrasts for the

---

[176] *Id.* at 385 (Judgment regarding atrocities).

[177] B. V. A. Roling, *Introduction, in* THE TOKYO WAR CRIMES TRIAL: AN INTERNATIONAL SYMPOSIUM 15, 17 (C. Hosoya, N. Ando, Y. Onuma, R. Minear, eds., 1986). Roling's thoughts are significant in that he was a jurist who sat on the IMTFE who cast several unsuccessful votes for acquittal.

[178] *Id.* at 16-17.

[179] *Id.* at 17 (quoting Ann & John Tusa).

benefit of future endeavors, he notes that he did not believe that the degree of any perceived unfairness warranted resignation.[180]

Notwithstanding this criticism, some scholars recognize the IMTFE as a positive, though flawed, exercise in post-conflict justice. The IMTFE operated in a considerably more difficult environment than did the IMT. The language barrier was much more pronounced, and as discussed above, the cultural gap was significant. Though imperfect in execution, the IMTFE is recognized as contributing to important developments in international law.

University of Vermont Professor Howard Ball cites the arguments made by Associate Justice Robert Jackson of the IMT to provide a defense to the claim that the IMTFE was simply victor's justice.[181] In the words of Justice Jackson, one must ask "whether law is so laggardly as to be utterly helpless to deal with crimes of this magnitude by criminals of this order of importance."[182] Notwithstanding the shortcomings of the IMTFE, Professor Ball notes that the contribution that the Tribunal made to the development and acceptance of "the principle of individual responsibility" was significant.[183]

---

[180] *Id.* at 19. Roling notes that he did disagree with several of the convictions and filed a dissenting opinion addressing his concerns. He went on to note that he voted for the acquittal of five of the accused and that with the passage of time, new evidence suggests to him that at least one of his votes for acquittal was in error. *Id.*

[181] It is not clear if Professor Ball shares Justice Jackson's support for the Tribunals. HOWARD BALL, PROSECUTING WAR CRIMES AND GENOCIDE: THE TWENTIETH-CENTURY EXPERIENCE 85 (U. Kan. Pr. 1999).

[182] *Id.* at 86.

[183] *Id.*

A recent account of the work of the IMTFE by Bradley University History Professor Tim Maga provides a significant counter-balance to the critics of the IMTFE.[184] Professor Maga directly notes that "[s]tanding in contrast to the concerns of its many critics, the Tokyo tribunal's commitment to justice and fair play continued to its ending days."[185] He notes that much of the criticism surrounding the IMTFE was directed at its chief prosecutor, Joseph Keenan, who was often alleged to have used the prosecution as a means to grandstand for higher political ends. Maga effectively argues to the contrary that Keenan was instead effectively building a record to preserve for history the atrocities committed by the Japanese.[186] Though Professor Maga recognizes that the trials "were flawed," he notes that the IMTFE's commitment to the "pursuit of justice" was "too quickly forgotten."[187]

The wide variance of opinion on the fairness of the IMTFE is much more extensive and overall more negative than the perceptions surrounding the IMT. The reasons for this are not clear, but there are lessons to be learned from the critiques. These include the recognition that significant language and cultural barriers may translate into perceptional problems for the court. Though not insurmountable, planners should take this factor into consideration as it might diminish the transparency of the court and thus undercut its legitimacy. Further, as much of the criticism of the IMTFE seams to be somewhat related to those selected for

---

[184] TIM MAGA, JUDGMENT AT TOKYO (U. Ky. Pr. 2001).

[185] *Id.* at 120.

[186] *Id.* at 121. Professor Maga notes that earlier writers also supported this position noting that many of its critics were "more concerned with minutia and procedural matters than with offenses against humanity." *Id.*

[187] *Id.* at 138.

service on the Tribunal and as prosecutors, great care should be taken in the selection of individuals to fill these positions.

5. Role of the Court as Part of Larger Reconstruction Plan

More so than in Germany, the IMTFE served as an introduction to procedures and processes consistent with the rule of law. The Tribunals were being conducted in an environment in which Supreme Allied Commander Douglas MacArthur sought to inculcate the values of an open judicial system even when recourse to the courts by the Japanese might result in the frustration of a particular policy of the occupation.[188]

Further, the undertaking in Japan required a complete reorientation of society and touched a myriad of activities of the civilian population often utilizing the official organs of government to the extent possible. On November 3, 1946, the Japanese Diet under the seal of the Emperor Hirohito brought to force a radical new constitution that ensured fundamental human rights to the population.[189] This document also established an independent judiciary,[190] and espoused a radical notion that sovereignty was now vested with and flowing from "the will of the people."[191]

6. Were the stated goals accomplished?

---

[188] I POLITICAL REORIENTATION OF JAPAN xx-xxi (1949) (introduction by Brigadier General Courtney).

[189] JAPAN CONST. ch. III, art. 10 (Nov. 3, 1946).

[190] *Id.* ch. IV.

[191] *Id.* ch. I, art. 1.

The IMTFE met a key goal of a justice system in that it served to fairly punish the wrongdoer. But the public display of trials of the principal Japanese war criminals served higher societal ends for the Japanese as well. In addition to punishment of the wrongdoer, the IMTFE served the dual purpose of educating the Japanese people as to the deeds of their government while providing a glimpse into a judicial system governed more by process and facts than desired outcome. Broader goals such as encouraging democratization and respect for human rights cannot be developed in a judicial vacuum. An independent judiciary is crucial for any lasting respect for such rights and the rule of law. Imperfect though it may have been, the IMTFE was the spark for a new Japanese legal order that has grown and endures today.

Further, in addition to the contributions the Tribunal made to the reestablishment of law, it was also part of a greater "political reorientation" of Japan that laid the foundation for a brighter future for Japan and its neighbors. The IMTFE was part of a comprehensive plan that brought justice and accountability to Japan, while developing democracy, encouraging respect for individual rights and the restoration of peace. A tremendous lesson learned from the work of the IMTFE is that a court of international justice can be a significant catalyst for justice and change. Japan was not only given the opportunity to have a judiciary constituted for it on paper in its Constitution, but was given a glimpse into a system governed by reason and process, not passion.

IV. The Use of National Military Commissions for the Prosecution of War Criminals

In addition to the International Military Tribunals, national military commissions have also been successful forums for the prosecution of war criminals. These military commissions played a significant role in the overall justice system as it related to war criminals during World War II.[192] Further, as with the International Tribunals, the national commissions served to meet the ends of justice while also demonstrating the rule of law in action to the affected populations. By doing so, these courts served key international objectives such as the restoration of peace and a contribution to the reconciliation of the belligerents. Reconciliation is furthered by the application of the rule of law as it serves to maximize the legitimacy and transparency of the process, while providing a forum for the prosecution of the instigators of unlawful war.

Trials conducted in the theater of operations by military commissions can meet similar national objectives. After World War II, the United States, British, Canadian and Australian Courts, among others, successfully mounted prosecutions against war criminals before their own military commissions.[193] As with International Military Tribunals, the exercise of this jurisdiction brings controversy. Where International Tribunals sought to bring major war criminals to justice and were integrated into a broader plan with goals such as democratization and the establishment of the rule of law, national commissions focused their

---

[192] The fundamental difference between an International Tribunal and a national military commission is that one is a creature of a multilateral international charter and the other is a creature of domestic law. Military commissions are courts of necessity that can meet the needs of justice in a variety of circumstances to include meting out punishment to war criminals, serious crimes committed by prisoners of war subject to key limitations imposed under international law, and can also fill the role of occupation courts. This article focuses on the use of military commissions for the punishment of war criminals.

[193] PATRICK BRODE, CASUAL SLAUGHTERS AND ACCIDENTAL JUDGMENTS: CANADIAN WAR CRIMES PROSECUTIONS, 1944-1948 xv (1997).

wrath and that of their populations upon lesser actors who often had committed a crime against one of the nationals of the prosecuting jurisdiction. The goals of these venues are more narrow and in the words of a Canadian legal scholar serve to illustrate that "there are restraints on warfare" and that "military excesses are morally unjustified and should be punished."[194]

The ability of these courts to provide a pressure valve for the civilian populations of the victors angered by war crimes committed against their soldiers does not necessarily reduce their effectiveness in facilitating the reconciliation of the former belligerents. To the contrary, when carefully constructed and properly executed they can further the restoration of peace by fixing accountability on the wrongdoers thus minimizing the depth of continued animosity directed toward the broader population. Wrath becomes focused on the perpetrators of the crime thus reducing a more generalized anger toward the population of the former enemy at large.

Further, these national military commissions serve important roles in the post-conflict environment by providing a forum to prosecute and punish war criminals whose conduct fell below the jurisdiction of the IMT and the IMTFE. This aspect of the use of military commissions serves an important function beyond those discussed above. Specifically, it serves to extend the reach of justice far beyond that of which a single international military tribunal is capable. Thus, the International Tribunals were able to focus on their prosecution of the major war criminals while relying on a responsive forum for the prosecution of lesser

---

[194] *Id.*

bad actors as well. As such, the past practice in the use of these forums can provide critical

insight into the successful development of a tailored system of post-conflict justice.

This section will focus on the use of military commissions to meet these goals by the

United States and Great Britain after World War II. Examples of cases that are reflective of

the breadth of the subject matter that these forums undertook as well as the procedures that

guided their work will be evaluated with a focus upon whether their use met the ends of

justice. Finally, this section will evaluate whether the procedures developed were just in

design and execution along with lessons learned from their triumphs and shortcomings.

A. Effectiveness of US Military Commissions for the Prosecution of War Criminals

The post-World War II prosecution of war criminals before United States military

commissions was and remains controversial.[195] These commissions were convened under the

authority of the Allied Control Council Law Number 10[196] in the American sector of

occupied Germany, and under regulations promulgated under the direction of Supreme

---

[195] One of the most controversial of these cases was *Ex parte Quirin*, 317 U.S. 1 (1942). The *Quirin* case involved the prosecution of Nazi saboteurs captured on United States soil by agents of the FBI. Though controversial, I have chosen to focus on war crimes trials that occurred outside of the United States as the focus of this piece is on the development of a post-conflict system of justice within a defeated nation after the cessation of active hostilities.

[196] Punishment of Persons Guilty of War Crimes, Crimes Against Peace and Against Humanity, Control Council Law No. 10 (December 20, 1945) [hereinafter Control Council Law No. 10]. The Control Council was an International Organization composed of representatives of the Allied powers. Control Council Law No. 10 was designed to "give effect to the terms of the Moscow Declaration . . . and in order to establish a uniform legal basis in Germany for the prosecution of war criminals and other similar offenders, other than those dealt with by the International Military Tribunal. . . ." *Id.*

Commander General Douglas MacArthur in the Pacific theater.[197] Though similar in key

procedural aspects, their planning and execution reflect marked differences. These

differences have led to a greater degree of criticism of the work of the commissions in the

Pacific over those conducted in Germany. The lessons learned by the United States in both

theaters after World War II, however, can provide a guide to improve the legitimacy of

commissions to the world today and in the future.[198]

1. United States Commissions in Germany

United States military commissions in the American Sector of Germany were authorized

by Control Council Law Number 10,[199] but their procedures were governed by local military

ordinance.[200] Further, though these courts were military commissions, they were officially

known as "Military Tribunals."[201] And though these were national courts as evidenced by

the way in which the cases were styled,[202] judge advocates at the time argued that they had an

international character. Most notably, Colonel Edward Ham Young stated that "[t]he

---

[197] General MacArthur expected to receive guidance from his superiors as to the procedures to conduct war crimes trials. Apparently preoccupied with developments in Germany, Washington failed to develop a coherent strategy for handling war criminals in the Far East that fell below the jurisdiction of the IMTFE. Ultimately, rather than develop regulations in Washington, they directed General MacArthur to develop the regulations locally. RICHARD L. LAEL, THE YAMASHITA PRECEDENT: WAR CRIMES AND COMMAND RESPONSIBILITY 59-61 (1982).

[198] For a discussion of lessons learned from the American and British experience with Military Commissions after World War II, *see infra* notes 199-237 and accompanying text.

[199] *See* Control Council Law No. 10, *supra* note 196.

[200] Organization and Powers of Certain Military Tribunals, Military Government-Germany, United States Zone, Ordinance Number 7 (October 18, 1946).

[201] *Id.* art. II.

[202] Courts convened under the authority of this ordinance were styled United States v. the pertinent defendant.

Nuernberg trials [conducted by the United States] were international in character. The Tribunals were not bound by technical rules of evidence as recognized by any jurisdiction of the United States of America . . . ."[203]

These military commissions in theory were not an extension or refinement of American courts-martial practice as developed under the Articles of War, but an entirely self contained set of procedural and evidentiary rules divorced entirely from any *controlling* body of American law apart from the rules developed by American lawyers under the auspices of Control Council Law Number 10.[204] In practice, however, they were products of an Anglo-American system of justice in which large quantities of evidence were gathered to meet high standards of proof but in an atmosphere of relaxed evidentiary standards. Many Germans were tried, many were acquitted and some were hanged.[205] But despite the pronouncement that the military commissions in Germany were outside the control of "any jurisdiction of the United States," in practice the cases before these commissions were similar to courts-martial with relaxed rules of evidence but a strong commitment to procedural fairness and the establishment of proof beyond a reasonable doubt before conviction.

---

[203] *Rules and Practice Concerning Various Types of Evidence: Introduction, in* XV Trial of War Criminals (Practice and Procedure) 627, 627 (Colonel Edward H. Young, ed., 1949).

[204] This stands in stark contrast to the approach taken by the British who conceived their commissions as an outgrowth of their military court-martial jurisprudence tailored to meet the exigencies of post war prosecutions. *See infra* notes 238-245 and accompanying text.

[205] For an exhaustive study of the use of documentary evidence at Nuremberg and a case by case list of convictions, acquittals and punishments adjudged to include executions, *see* JOHN MENDELSOHN, TRIAL BY DOCUMENT: THE USE OF SEIZED RECORDS IN THE UNITED STATES PROCEEDINGS AT NUERNBERG (Garland 1988).

The case of *United States v. Brandt, et al.*[206] provides a good example. The *Brandt* case, known collectively as the *Medical Cases,* involved the trial of key personnel within the Nazi medical establishment. This community was led by Professor Doctor Karl Brandt who held the rank of Lieutenant General in the Waffen SS.[207] He was also appointed "General Commissioner for Medical and Health matters" with the "highest Reich authority."[208] The *Medical Cases* involved the investigation and trial of Nazi physicians who had been tasked to conduct a wide range of medical experiments on human subjects. The experiments at the center of the trial can be broadly classed as follows: the sulfanilamide experiments;[209] freezing; malaria; bone, muscle and nerve regeneration; bone transplantation; sea water drinking; sterilization; typhus;[210] jaundice vaccine experimentation;[211] mustard gas protection medication experiments;[212] and medical euthanasia.[213]

The greatest criticism of the conduct of the American military commissions in Germany is similar to that often leveled against the IMT – the heavy reliance on the use of

---

[206] United States v. Brandt, et al., I-II Tr. Of War Crim bef. the Nuernberg Mil. Trib. 1 (1947). As the case spans two volumes of reporters, the long form will be used for case citation for clarity.

[207] *Id.* at 190.

[208] Decree of Adolf Hitler, Appointment of Dr. Karl Brandt (August 25, 1944), *cited at* United States v. Brandt, et al., I-II Tr. Of War Crim bef. the Nuernberg Mil. Trib. 1, 191 (1947).

[209] These experiments involved injecting infection into test subjects to test the effectiveness of sulfanilamide drugs. At least three subjects died. United States v. Brandt, et al., II Tr. Of War Crim bef. the Nuernberg Mil. Trib. 1, 193 (1947) (findings of the court).

[210] *Id.* at 195.

[211] *Id.* at 194.

[212] *Id.*

[213] *Id.* at 196.

documentary evidence. In the *Medical Cases*, the prosecution introduced 570 exhibits, with the Defense taking advantage of the relaxed rules to submit 904 of their own.[214] The criticism cuts both ways, however. The prosecution may be able to introduce a large quantity of documents in support of the case, but the defense could also benefit as they generally will be in a better position to identify the location of documents and other material that may tend to exculpate them while maintaining no duty to identify the location of inculpatory evidence for the prosecutors.

The cases before the United States commissions were also well defended in both their factual development and legal argument. Unlike the experience of defendants before most other commissions, those before the United States Tribunal at Nuernberg were individually represented in most cases by experienced German attorneys.[215] The defense counsel before the Court were key in counterbalancing what may have become a show trial in light of the relaxed evidentiary standards. The defense counsel before these courts, however, were successful in sparing many clients from death, mitigating the punishment for others and obtaining acquittals for a substantial number.[216] Thus, while clearly helping their clients, they also served the important societal end of ensuring the legitimate execution of justice.

---

[214] JOHN MENDELSOHN, TRIAL BY DOCUMENT: THE USE OF SEIZED RECORDS IN THE UNITED STATES PROCEEDINGS AT NURNBERG 208 (Garland 1988).

[215] For example, in one case there were in excess of 90 defense counsel involved in the defense of twenty-one defendants with several other "Special Counsel" available for the accused. The sole non-German attorney was from the United States. *Id*. at 194-99.

[216] In the *Medical Cases*, there were twenty-three defendants in the dock. Of these, seven were sentenced to death with a like number of acquittals. The remaining nine were sentenced to periods of years ranging from ten years to life. This was typical of the cases before the Court with many cases resulting in no sentences of death

The defense also had success in shaping the legal battlefield. Defense counsel challenged the entire legal underpinning of the court's procedures and jurisdiction on various theories based on German and international law. For example, the defense representing Dr. Karl Brandt argued that the affidavits used against his client should be inadmissible to the extent that they were obtained from interrogations conducted by someone other than a Judge.[217] He made similar mixed arguments based on restrictions arising from German law that had not been properly interfaced with the Control Council regulation,[218] and argued that international law could not pierce what the state said should be done to its own citizens as part of medical experimentation for the greater good.[219] The arguments were tightly reasoned and well constructed.[220]

Brandt's defense, however, is in some respect a tribute to the overall quality of the evidence presented. While he put up a vigorous defense on the merits to many of the charges he was facing, he was ultimately acquitted of many as the commission found that the evidence did "not show beyond a reasonable doubt" that he had the requisite criminal knowledge of some of the medical experiments being conducted in medical commands under

---

and many acquittals. For an excellent statistical analysis of the results of the trials before this United States commission, *see id.* at 175-90.

[217] United States v. Brandt, et al., II Tr. Of War Crim bef. the Nuernberg Mil. Trib. 1, 123-4 (1947) (argument of defense counsel Dr. Servatius).

[218] *Id.* at 124.

[219] *Id.* at 127-29.

[220] Of course, as with all criminal cases, client control can become an issue. One would like to think this was the case when Dr. Poppendick gave his final statement. He stated that he joined the SS not because he wanted to do evil, but because he was an "idealist." Poppendick thought his work at the "Main Race and Settlement Office" as positive work for the family. *Id.* at 155. His comments seem to reflect the series of events that brought ultimate destruction to Germany.

his authority. Though he was acquitted of these charges, the commission found that "he certainly knew that medical experiments were carried out . . . [that] caused suffering, injury, and death."[221]

Brandt, however, was convicted of numerous other charges including some in which high level correspondence indicated that he had participated in activities that he denied.[222] Much of the defense, however, did not involve a denial of the underlying facts which appeared to be accepted in the face of overwhelming evidence. This was the case with respect to Brandt's role in Germany's euthanasia program. His defense was simply that his conduct reflected bad political morals, not a crime, and perhaps that his conduct was in fact noble.[223] The Court was not so moved, and returned a finding of guilty for a variety of offenses and a sentence of death.[224]

2. United States Commissions in the Pacific

As discussed above, General MacArthur's legal staff was left to their own devices to develop the regulations to govern the prosecution of war criminals before military commissions in the Far East. This undertaking, though done in haste, was carried out in a

---

[221] *Id.* at 195 (judgment of the court).

[222] *See, e.g.,* findings related to the Jaundice Experiments in which the Court relied on letters penned by Brandt requesting that prisoners be provided for experimentation. *Id.* at 194.

[223] *Id.* at 134.

[224] *Id.* at 189-98. The *Medical Case* could play itself out again in modern times. Evidence exists to suggest that Iraq conducted experiments on prisoners to further their biological weapons program. Over 1600 prisoners participated in these experiments that resulted in the mass death of the prisoners. *Presentation of Secretary of State Colin Powell to the United Nations Security Council* (CNBC television broadcast, February 5, 2003).

professional manner with his Judge Advocates studying and borrowing from an eclectic body

of law. These sources of law included British Regulations that governed war crimes

prosecutions,[225] the *Quirin* decision and various Army Regulations and field manuals.[226]

Consistent with the approach adopted by the International Military Tribunals and other

United States and Allied commissions, the most striking deviation from traditional military

practice of the day was in the evidentiary standards.[227] The commission was directed to

"admit such evidence as in its opinion would be of assistance in proving or disproving the

charge, or such as in the commission's opinion would have probative value in the mind of the

reasonable man."[228] From this general guidance, the applicable rules of evidence permitted

the court to consider official documents,[229] documents from the International Red Cross,[230]

"affidavits, depositions, or other statements" taken by proper military authority,[231] and diaries

---

[225] *See infra* notes 238-245 and accompanying text.

[226] *See Ex parte Quirin*, 317 U.S. 1 (1942) and RICHARD L. LAEL, THE YAMASHITA PRECEDENT: WAR CRIMES AND COMMAND RESPONSIBILITY 66 (1982).

[227] For example, a review of legal issues reviewed arising from courts-martial during World War II reveals that while the procedures were similar, courts-martial were guided by traditional notions of evidence typical of common law jurisdictions. Legal issues identified in a series of rape case are similar to those encountered today such as the use of prior inconsistent statements, multiplicity, character evidence and hearsay. *See* II DIGEST OF OPINIONS OF THE EUROPEAN THEATER OF OPERATIONS 439-60 (1945).

[228] In re Yamashita, 66 S. Ct. 340, 363 n. 9 (1946) (dissent of J. Rutledge) (citing sec. 16 of the Rules of Procedure).

[229] *Id.* sec. 16(a)(1).

[230] *Id.* sec 16(a)(2).

[231] *Id.* sec. 16(a)(3).

or any other document "appearing to the commission to contain information related to the charge."[232]

As with the British,[233] the United States in the Pacific selected a case with import to an American possession – the Philippines – to serve as the first case tried before military commission. The case of General Yamashita immortalized before the United States Supreme Court in *In re Yamashita* involved the prosecution of the commander of Japanese forces in the Philippines for war crimes. His highly criticized prosecution was based in part upon a theory of command responsibility in that he knew or should have known of the atrocities committed by soldiers under his command because of the scope of his troop's activity.[234]

Though the underlying strength of the Supreme Court's ruling that served to legitimize the prosecution's efforts is beyond the scope of this paper, the case is helpful in evaluating the conduct of the case by the commission itself. A close review of the matter reveals that the legitimacy of the outcome of the case is damaged less from the procedures ratified than from the method of execution. Specifically, the case was moved forward at a rapid pace and efforts by the defense to challenge the evidence presented by the government was greatly restricted by the court.

---

[232] *Id.* sec. 16(a)(4).

[233] *See infra* note 273 and accompanying text.

[234] For a good discussion of the *Yamashita* case from the perspective of the defense, *see generally* RICHARD L. LAEL, THE YAMASHITA PRECEDENT: WAR CRIMES AND COMMAND RESPONSIBILITY (1982).

By any standard, the trial of General Yamashita moved briskly. General Yamashita surrendered to Allied custody on September 3, 1945 and was served with war crimes charges on September 25. Thirteen days later he was arraigned at which time he entered a plea of not guilty. After unsuccessful attempts to obtain delays, the case began in earnest on October 29, 1945 and continued until findings were announced on Pearl Harbor Day – December 7, 1945. On that day, the Court returned a guilty finding and sentenced General Yamashita to death by hanging.[235]

The trial of General Yamashita highlights the potential frailty of any system of justice when the court fails to follow the spirit of the law in practice. As noted above, the problem with the trial of General Yamashita was less about weaknesses in the procedures, but in their execution.[236] When viewed with the benefit of history, *In re Yamashita* appears more about a race to conclude a case before Pearl Harbor Day than a model for jurists seeking to oversee commissions.

Unfortunately, though many commissions followed that of General Yamashita, it became the symbol of American justice in the Pacific to the outside world. Thus, while the prosecution was upheld by the United States Supreme Court, it has faired less well over time in the minds of the public. This experience, coupled with those of the American

---

[235] In re Yamashita, 66 S. Ct. 340, 343 (1946).

[236] The procedures developed for use by American commissions were based in part upon the British regulations that were used successfully in both theaters of operation. *See supra* notes 225-226 and accompanying text.

commissions in Germany and the British experience discussed below provide valuable insights into the future development and use of these forums.[237]

B. British Prosecutions Before Military Commissions

The British actively prosecuted war criminals – both military and civilian – before military commissions in Europe and the Asian-Pacific theatre. The procedures that governed the conduct of war crimes trials were based heavily on their system of courts-martial. The regulations prescribing the conduct of a British court-martial were incorporated into the procedures for use in the trial of war criminals "[e]xcept in so far as herein otherwise provided expressly or by implication."[238] The greatest variance from the procedures employed for the trial of British soldiers came in the area of admissibility of evidence.

As with the procedures employed by the IMT and IMTFE, the British war crimes regulation relaxed evidentiary standards in the face of the post-conflict realities encountered. These relaxed rules permitted the admission of statements "made by or attributable" to someone who is dead or otherwise "unable to attend or give evidence."[239] Likewise, official Allied and Axis government documents "signed or issued officially" were deemed self-authenticating without further proof[240] as were reports made by a wide variety of

---

[237] *See infra* notes 238-250 and accompanying text.

[238] Regulations for the Trial of War Criminals (United Kingdom), art. 3, June 18, 1945 [hereinafter UK War Crimes Regulation].

[239] *Id.* art. 8(i)(a).

[240] *Id.* art. 8(i)(b).

nongovernmental actors to include medical doctors and members of the International Red Cross.[241] Other evidence deemed of sufficient quality for a relaxed admission standard included transcripts from any other military court,[242] or contents extracted from "any diary, letter or other document appearing to contain information relating to the charge."[243] Lastly, if any documents had been seen by a witnesses but were subsequently lost, the commission could entertain testimony concerning the contents of any admissible original document that was otherwise unavailable.[244]

These relaxed evidentiary standards broadly expanded the ability of the court to receive evidence that would have otherwise been inadmissible under British rules. The regulations explicitly acknowledged this and cautioned the Court of its "duty . . . to judge the weight to be attached to any evidence given in pursuance of this Regulation that would not otherwise be admissible."[245] Notwithstanding these relaxed rules, a review of the British Commission's results reveals that they discharged their duties with due regard to process and the rights of accused brought before them.

The Commissions were not show trials with seemingly predetermined results. To the contrary, the verdicts handed down by the British Commissions reflect the willingness to

---

[241] *Id.* art. 8(i)(c).

[242] *Id.* art. 8(i)(d).

[243] UK War Crimes Regulation, *supra* note 238, art. 8(i)(e).

[244] *Id.* art. 8(i)(f).

[245] *Id.* art. 8(i).

apply high standards of proof in an environment characterized by relaxed standards of evidence. Accordingly, the courts served several often-competing interests in post-conflict justice. The British Commissions served to fix responsibility upon the wrongdoer, contribute to the reestablishment of the rule of law while de-legitimizing the horrendous conduct of the actors, and ultimately providing accountability necessary in order to transition from war to peace.

The trials of war criminals before British Commissions concerned themselves in many cases with conduct that by international standards of then and now were *malum in se*.[246] As one commentator noted with respect to one historic British Commission: "the trial did not represent any drastic innovation [in international law]" but the perceived "novelty" of the trial was more a result of "extraordinary and unprecedented character of the offenses resulting from the conduct of war by the military and political leaders of National-Socialist Germany."[247]

The crimes – murder, torture, kidnapping – were well known in the individual and collective laws of nations, but they were conducted on a scale that seemed to transform them into a new type of conduct beyond the pale of the law. The British approach, as with others adopted nationally and internationally, served to forge new expansive procedures to capture and punish the wrongdoing of others committed as part of an internationalized criminal

---

[246] "A crime or act that is inherently immoral, such as murder, arson, or rape." BLACK'S LAW DICTIONARY 971 (7th ed. 1999).

[247] H. Lauterpacht, *Foreword, in* VII WAR CRIMES TRIALS SERIES xiii (George Brand, ed., London, William Hodge & Co. Ltd. 1950) (commenting on the "*Velpke Baby Home Trial*").

movement of unprecedented scale. In essence, they were cases of common, albeit serious, crimes perpetuated on a horrific scale.

An understanding of the British approach can be developed through looking at three cases with well developed records from two different theaters of operations. From Europe, the case by the British against Heinrich Gerike and others known as the *Velpke Baby Home Tria"*[248] and from Asia, the trial of *Gozawa Sadaichi and nine others,*[249] and the so-called *Double Tenth Trial*[250] are instructive on the British approach to the trial of war criminals before national commissions.

1. British Commissions in Germany

The *Velpke Baby Home Trial* is interesting for two distinct reasons. First, the trial was principally concerned with civilian responsibility for war crimes committed on behalf of the state. Second, the case was an early attempt to define the nature and scope of universal jurisdiction since it included criminal conduct that extended beyond the borders of Germany proper.[251] Though the trial was held in Brunswick, Germany by the British, it involved crimes that were committed in part in Poland while occupied by Germany.

---

[248] The King v. Heinrich Gerike, *et al*, VII Trial of War Criminals 1 (1946).

[249] The King v. Gozawa Sadaichi and Nine Others, III Trial of War Criminals 1 (1946).

[250] In re Lt. Col. Sumida Haruzo and 20 Others, *reported in* THE DOUBLE TENTH TRIAL: WAR CRIMES COURT (Bashir A. Mallal, ed., The Malayan Law Journal Office, 1947).

[251] H. Lauterpacht, *Foreward, in* VII WAR CRIMES TRIALS SERIES xiii (George Brand, ed., London, William Hodge & Co. Ltd. 1950)(commenting on the "Velpke Baby Home Trial"). Professor Lauterpacht defines

The *Velpke Baby Home Trial* developed out of a German operation in occupied Poland in 1944 and was related to the use of female Polish slave laborers in the German agricultural sector in Germany proper.[252] The recipients of the slave laborers – German farmers charged with the difficult task of supporting the agricultural needs of the German war machine – began to complain that their Polish slaves were prone to pregnancy and thus were "substantially interfering with the agricultural work output for the German war effort."[253] In response to these complaints, the NSDAP[254] directed that eastern slave women were prohibited from marriage or procreation, and that any offspring of such women were "rendered illegitimate by German law."[255] These children were then forcibly taken from their mothers and placed in the custody of a children's home. The mothers were then returned to the fields and the babies were sent to what became known as the "Velpke barracks."[256]

The baby home proved to be woefully inadequate for the care of the children confined there with poor staffing and medical treatment. As a result, during an eight month period ending in December 1944, ninety-six of 110 children sent to the home died of neglect and

---

"universality of jurisdiction" as "jurisdiction independent of the locality of the crime or of the nationality of the offender or victims. . . ." *Id.*

[252] The King v. Heinrich Gerike, *et al*, VII Trial of War Criminals 1, 3 (1946) (Opening Speech for the Prosecution).

[253] *Id.*

[254] *Id.* at 4. NSDPA is the German acronym for is the National German Socialist Workers' Party.

[255] *Id.*

[256] *Id.* at 5.

maltreatment.[257] Upon death, the bodies of the children were secreted away and buried in unmarked graves. The prosecution contended that the mass neglect of these children demonstrated that "these children were never meant to live" and as a result were subjected to "willful neglect" calculated to result in their death.[258]

Though this commission was focused ultimately on the individual criminal conduct of civilians, the case proceeded as a violation of the laws of war, not as a violation of domestic law. The indictment of the various defendants was hinged upon a violation of international law in that it was contrary to the Hague Rules of 1907 which prohibited, *inter alia*, inhumane treatment of populations living under occupation and crimes against the "family rights and private property rights of civilians in occupied countries."[259] The prosecution also supported its indictment by arguing that customary international law forbad the deportation of slave labor or the intentional killing of innocent civilians.[260]

Thus the indictment alleged that the defendants were "charged with committing a war crime . . . [by the] killing by willful neglect of a number of children, Polish nationals."[261] The indictment alleged violations against eight individuals that represented the planners,

---

[257] The King v. Heinrich Gerike, *et al*, VII Trial of War Criminals 1, 6 (1946) (Opening Speech for the Prosecution).

[258] *Id*. at 7. The prosecution noted that "medical attention" was generally limited to the "sign[ing] of death certificates." *Id*.

[259] *Id*. at 8 (citing Hague Treaty, 1907, art. 45-46).

[260] *Id*. This concept the use of slave labor was in violation of international law appears throughout the practice of the international tribunals and national commissions. *See, e.g.*, IMTFE CHARTER, supra note 145, art. 5(c) that prohibits the "enslavement" of civilian populations.

[261] The King v. Heinrich Gerike, *et al*, VII Trial of War Criminals 1, 3 (1946) (citing the arraignment).

operators and medical personnel of the home.[262] Half were acquitted, with the others

convicted and sentenced to punishments ranging from ten years to two sentences of death.[263]

While the *Velpke Baby Home Trial* represents the use of military commissions to try

civilians for committing war crimes against non-nationals, the case against *Gozawa Sadaichi*

and nine others[264] demonstrates the use of such forum to bring accountability upon soldiers

who abuse prisoners of war (POW) subject to their control. Though the *Gozawa* trial stems

from activity within the Asian theater of operations, the regulations that governed their

execution were the same as those used in Europe.[265]

2. British Commissions in the Pacific

The trial of war criminals by the British in Asia were subject to two key local policies,

however, that served to restrict their use. First, no trial was to be pursued unless there was

"irrefutable" proof of guilt and identity.[266] This restriction was deemed critical to the British

---

[262] *Id.*

[263] *Id.* at 342-343 (citing from the announcements of sentences).

[264] The King v. Gozawa Sadaichi and Nine Others, III Trial of War Criminals 1 (1946).

[265] *See supra* notes 238-245 and accompanying text.

[266] Rear-Admiral the Rt Hon. Earl Mountbatten of Burma, *Foreword, in* III WAR CRIMES TRIALS SERIES xiii (George Brand, ed., London, William Hodge & Co. Ltd. 1950) (commenting on the command philosophy with respect to the trial of war criminals before British military commissions). Notwithstanding the requirement of "irrefutable" proof as a prerequisite to the initiation of charges, Commissions had no problem finding the lack of such proof on findings with respect to both guilt and identity. This reflected a great sensitivity to the perception of the commission in the eyes of the local population and the broader international community. Though the evidentiary standards of admissibility were greatly relaxed, cases such as the Gozawa trial indicate that these relaxed standards did not translate into a relaxed burden of proof. *See infra* notes 274-283 and accompanying text.

command in South East Asia so as to prevent the "diminish[ment] of our prestige [by] appear[ing] to be instigating vindictive trials against enemies of a beaten enemy nation . . . ." [267] Second, to further minimize the appearance of opportunistic prosecutions, trials were only authorized when upon reflection it appeared that "a sentence of seven years or more was likely to be inflicted . . . ."[268] Those whose cases upon evaluation appeared to warrant less punishment were released.[269] Further, the *Gozawa* case is illustrative in that it reveals the extent to which the court and its scholarly contemporaries used the procedural backdrop of British law to fill the gaps left in the regulation governing the trial of war criminals.[270]

Gozawa Sadaichi was a company commander in charge of Indian prisoners of war and was responsible for their care and administration in a movement that began in Singapore and ended with their arrival and incarceration at Babelthuap.[271] Upon arrival at Babelthuap, Captain Gozawa became responsible for the Indian prisoners interned in the island's prisoner of war camp to include establishing the methods of POW camp regulation and discipline. The regulations and their implementation were the focus of the *Gozawa* trial because they

---

[267] *Id.* at xiii-xiv.

[268] *Id.* at xiv.

[269] *Id.*

[270] *See supra* notes 238-245 and accompanying text.

[271] The period of time covered by this commission was from May 1943 when the transport of the POWs began and September 1945 when the camp was liberated by the United States armed forces. *See Introduction, in* III WAR CRIMES TRIALS SERIES xxxii (George Brand, ed., London, William Hodge & Co. Ltd. 1950).

resulted in numerous deaths of Indian POWs as a result of malnutrition, torture and execution. [272]

Cases such as these were unfortunately all too common, yet the *Gozawa* trial was to assume a key position in the history of international justice. The *Gozawa* trial was the first commission tried by the British in Asia. History provides an unsigned explanation contained in the introduction to the official report of the trial that provides:

> The real reason must be sought far from the crowded atmosphere of Singapore and indeed, far from the scene of Malaya itself. At the end of 1945 there were being conducted in far-away India, a number of trials of leaders of the Indian National Army, that force which had been encouraged and assisted by the Japanese to fight against British arms during the period of Japanese occupation. These trials were attended by demonstrations of disorder in a greater or less degree, and became enshrouded with that atmosphere of political significance which it seems to be inseparable, in India, from any trial of public interest. It was thought, therefore, that this was an excellent moment to launch upon the world a trial in which Indians were the victims, and to demonstrate once more the absolute equality before the law of the rights of all Imperial subjects, irrespective of nationality, race or colour.[273]

Thus the palpable interest of the British in pursuing the trial of Gozawa was of a domestic nature. It reflected the desire of the British government to both punish those who had committed law of war violations against their forces while also seeking to satisfy domestic ends with their Indian subjects. But while this commission was convened in part to meet domestic political aims, it was not a show trial. Further, notwithstanding the local guidance

---

[272] The King v. Gozawa Sadaichi and Nine Others, III Trial of War Criminals 1, 203-05 (1946).

[273] *Introduction, in* III WAR CRIMES TRIALS SERIES xlii (George Brand, ed., London, William Hodge & Co. Ltd. 1950).

that such trials could only go forward upon the existence of irrefutable proof,[274] the

Commission found the failure of such proof with respect to one of the defendants and

acquitted him.[275]

The evidence that was used to convict the remaining defendants appears to have met the

local pretrial standard of irrefutable proof. In face of such proof, the main thrust of the

defense was not based upon disputing the facts, but the legal basis of the procedure in

question as well as other affirmative defenses.[276] These defenses included arguments that it

was impossible to better care for the Indian POWs under the circumstances,[277] that the actors

were obeying orders,[278] that the Japanese were not bound to respect POWs as they did not

sign the International Convention Relative to the Treatment of Prisoners of War, 1929,[279] or

in the alternative that the Indians were not prisoners of war.[280] The defense also argued that

---

[274] *See supra* notes 266-269.

[275] The King v. Gozawa Sadaichi and Nine Others, III Trial of War Criminals 1, 227 (1946). The court was not particularly impressed with Sergeant Major Ono Tadasu whom they described as possessing a mind "steeped with blind and brutish obedience." *Id.* Yet the court informed him that the allegations had not "been proved to the necessity according to British Law." *Id.*

[276] One key exception to this observation is that the defense did make an argument that the charge of murdering one Sapoy Mohamed Shafi could not stand because of a failure of proof – namely that his body was never produced. Though this argument was based upon a theory of factual insufficiency, at its core was a defense based upon law as the defense acknowledged that there was some evidence based on witnesses that a murder had occurred. *Id.* at 206-07.

[277] *Id.* at 210.

[278] *Id.* at 221.

[279] *Id.* at 224.

[280] *Id.* This argument flows from the position that these Indians were actually traitors against the British and had joined the Japanese forces. This was a thinly developed defense.

the Court should use its power to consider the appropriate weight to give to the sworn affidavits submitted under the circumstances.[281]

The approach forged by the defense coupled with many key concessions such as "the fact that Nakamura executed Shafi there can, of course, be no doubt . . . he has admitted it himself"[282] reflects the desire of the prosecution to bring only cases of irrefutable proof. But if the command made a misstep and moved a case forward without solid proof, the British Commissions responded accordingly. Such cases reveal the willingness of the Commissions to acquit when the Court found that the prosecutors had failed to prove that particular defendants had committed "any particular act of ill-treatment against anybody."[283]

Such was the case in the *Double Tenth* trial in which the Court acquitted several of the co-accused for reasons of severe to slight failures of proof.[284] The *Double Tenth* trial was so named because it stemmed in part from a mass atrocity committed against British civilians on 10 October 1943. These British civilians had been rounded up in Singapore and kept in the Changi Jail near Singapore Harbor. After a few transistor radio receivers were discovered

---

[281] *Id.* at 213.

[282] *Id.* at 221. This concession is particularly interesting in light of the legal defense cited above that a conviction for the murder of Shafi could not be obtained because of lack of sufficient evidence of a body. *See supra* note 276.

[283] In re Lt. Col. Sumida Haruzo and 20 Others, *reported in* THE DOUBLE TENTH TRIAL: WAR CRIMES COURT 587 (Bashir A. Mallal, ed., The Malayan Law Journal Office, 1947).

[284] This case reflects the great efforts that the British commissions would go to ensure that all convictions would be supported by the evidence. This was true even when it was clear that the Court had nothing but disregard for the accused before the bar. Often the court would lecture the accused prior to announcing their acquittal. The speech to acquitted accused Sergeant Major Sugimoto is instructive. In the words of the Court, "[t]he Court heard the evidence which you gave in the witness-box, and has come to the conclusion that you were lying from the beginning to the end, but lies do not make a man guilty of a war crime." *Id.*

and their British possessors tortured and executed, the Japanese became suspicious that the British civilians were secretly transmitting intelligence from the jail. Though untrue, these suspicions were "confirmed" when the Australians successfully raided a Japanese ship laying off the coast. This triggered a round of torture and execution of British civilians.

One survivor of this round up, The Honorable Mr. Justice N. A. Worley, recalls that they had been called to a routine formation punctuated by "the sudden and unexpected appearance of armed sentries and of repulsive looking men" who "were 'acting on information received'".[285] Though the legal issues facing the Court were similar to those faced by the cases cited above, this case is particularly illustrative of the extent to which these Commissions would go to ensure that burdens of *proof* were not relaxed in an environment characterized by relaxed rules of evidence. Though defendants were part of an organized activity of brutality and death, the Court required that the evidence presented on individuals establish their guilt and that the evidence admitted through the relaxed evidentiary procedures be corroborated to ensure reliability.

Some of the acquittals resulted from the Court finding mistaken identity in the affirmative. These cases were less a failure of proof and more an affirmative finding by the Commission that the accused before it was factually not guilty. Others of the acquitted, however, appeared to be guilty but not to the satisfaction of the Court who would resolve conflicting evidence to the benefit of the accused. For example, the court acquitted Private

---

[285] N. A. Worley, *Foreword, in* THE DOUBLE TENTH TRIAL: WAR CRIMES COURT xi, xi (Bashir A. Mallal, ed., The Malayan Law Journal Office, 1947) (Justice Worley was not quoting a specific individual in his comments).

Murata Yoshitaro because the prosecution relied on a single affidavit of a prisoner with corroboration coming from what appeared to be an incriminating photograph.

The defense strategy was to call into question the identity of the person in the photograph in an effort to reduce the evidence against his client to that of an uncorroborated affidavit. The strategy worked. The Court in announcing its findings with respect to Murata appeared frustrated by its acquittal noting that they had "good reason to believe that it was [Murata]" in the photograph but finding that the state of the evidence was "insufficient . . . to convict . . . ."[286] Commissions such as the *Double Tenth* trial stand for the proposition that the rule of law can and must carry the day even under difficult circumstances. It also demonstrates that seasoned jurists can conduct trials in which relaxed evidentiary standards are permitted without compromising the required burden of proof beyond a reasonable doubt.

C. Perceptions of Fairness and Lessons Learned from the World War II Commissions

The modern view of the fairness and effectiveness of the national commissions after World War II are mixed. Military commissions operate in a difficult environment and must balance many competing interests to include: the needs of society to punish the wrongdoer; the needs of society to ensure compliance with the rule of law and the protection of those brought before the Courts and ultimately the need for the justice system to further, not detract from, the ultimate reconciliation of the belligerents.

---

[286] In re Lt. Col. Sumida Haruzo and 20 Others, *reported in* THE DOUBLE TENTH TRIAL: WAR CRIMES COURT 587 (Bashir A. Mallal, ed., The Malayan Law Journal Office, 1947).

A study of the American and British commissions in Germany and the Pacific after World War II provides a wealth of insight and information. These experiences support the following conclusions: relaxed rules of evidence do not necessarily compromise the validity of results; corroboration of evidence of a traditionally inadmissible nature is important to ensuring legitimate results; and, the best practicable evidence should be used rather than permitting relaxed evidentiary standards to substitute for otherwise available evidence of a more traditional nature. Lastly, superior defense counsel coupled with adequate time to prepare is critical for the development of a record that will withstand current and future scrutiny.

The relaxed rules of evidence authorized by the various regulations discussed above did not compromise the validity of the trials as it is clear that the Jurists involved did not interpret this relaxed evidentiary standard as a departure from the traditional burdens of proof in a criminal trial. This can be seen in the regulatory admonishment to properly weigh such evidence by the British[287] as well as the practice by their commissions to seek corroborating evidence to support such evidence.[288] Further, it is important that the defense be provided the same ability to introduce such evidence as was clearly the case in law and practice before the United States Commissions in Germany.[289]

---

[287] *See supra* note 245 and accompanying text.

[288] *See supra* notes 285-286 and accompanying text.

[289] *See supra* note 214 and accompanying text.

Perhaps the greatest lesson of these commissions, however, is the need for highly qualified and individual defense counsel for the accused. These counsel can come from the nation of the accused, the nation of the commission, or both. The Court must ensure, however, that the representation is effective and that it is given the time and resources necessary to presenting its best defense. It is of crucial importance as these courts serve not only for a forum for the punishment of the wrongdoer, but also as an introduction of the rule of law and due process to societies historically plagued by the yoke of totalitarianism. These courts play a key initial role in the public inculcation of the value and importance of the individual – even criminals.

The World War II military commissions served important roles in meeting both their nations' need for justice and the needs of the local civilian population to see the rule of law in action while learning of the atrocities that brought the war to their communities.[290] These forums can serve similar roles in the future. They should always be considered as a tool available to legal and government planners faced with the daunting task of developing a post-conflict judicial system capable of meeting both the traditional needs of justice and the overarching goal of societal reconstruction and reconciliation.

---

[290] Even in the era of cable television and the internet, the mass civilian populations of totalitarian regimes often must rely solely on state owned news organizations for news. For example, prior to the regime change in Iraq, the state ensured that there was a news blackout to prevent coverage of key diplomatic releases that challenged the Iraqi regime's conduct. *Fox News Alert: Awaiting Powell Address to UN RE: Iraq Weapons* (Fox News Channel television broadcast, Feb. 5, 2003).

V. The Overarching Goals of Reconciliation & Restoration of Peace

This section will analyze how a system of post-conflict justice can aid or hinder the ultimate goal of reconciliation of the belligerents. Three areas will be considered. First, the role that post-conflict justice can and should take in complementing the overall efforts to restore peace, provide order in the society and as a process that serves the ends of reconciliation. Second, the lessons from modern truth and reconciliation commissions that can serve to aid in the reconciliation of diverse domestic populations that have been subject to various sources of violence. And third, the effectiveness of modern models for fixing responsibility for war crimes while simultaneously serving the ends of reconciliation and the restoration of peace.

A. Post-Conflict Reconciliation and the Long Term Restoration of Peace

The trial of war criminals before various international, national and domestic forums can serve the interests of justice and compliment the ultimate goal of the reconciliation of the belligerents and the restoration of peace.[291] Lessons from World War II indicate that these interests will be served if the procedures are open to public scrutiny, and serve to provide a full accounting of the state's criminal conduct as exercised through its agents. This full accounting can only be accomplished if the procedures adopted in practice serve to ensure a full and complete defense by the accused.

---

[291] The focus of this work will be in situations where the end of the belligerency results in the collapse or termination of the former regime followed by a period of occupation or other arrangement in which the vanquished is placed under interim management by a transnational governing body.

Further, these ends are not served by developing an "on the shelf" solution that can be deployed at the end of any conflict characterized by atrocities. To the contrary, a post-conflict system of justice needs to be tailored to meet the needs of the unique populations and constituencies that present themselves. Failure to do so will miss an opportunity to reconcile competing interests while possibly setting the stage for future international armed conflict or civil war.

This aspect of a post-conflict system of justice can be best understood by the recognition that different forums for prosecution serve different and often competing ends. After World War II, the International Military Tribunals served several functions for the broader international community, the parties and victims of the belligerency, and the underlying domestic populations of the vanquished. For the international community, the Tribunals sent a message of deterrence that prosecutors of unlawful wars and instigators of crimes against humanity would be held accountable by the world community while simultaneously providing a forum for bringing a final accountability of the defeated nation's crimes.[292]

These tribunals also served the domestic needs of the victorious parties to the conflict by subjecting the principals of an unlawful war characterized by mass atrocities to justice. This process of accountability – as with a traditional criminal case – can serve to reduce the animosity of the civilian populations of the belligerency harmed by the unlawful acts of the principals. By fixing responsibility at the leadership, the injured populations can receive the

---

[292] It is the author's opinion that this general deterrent affect borders on the illusory in preventing hostility. This precedent, however, may in some circumstances serve to end a hostility early as part of an amnesty deal. It may also serve to deter other bad conduct if the state perpetrator perceives that the world may invade his borders to apprehend him for crimes against humanity if his conduct does not cease.

psychological benefits of the justice system while the process serves to prevent the return of the bad actors to power.

As important, however, are the needs of the civilian populations of the vanquished that can be served by such international tribunals. First, when conducted in an open forum calculated to develop a full accountability, the domestic population can come to understand the scope of the atrocities that played a part in the decision of the victors to go to war. Further, societies that have not known the rule of law can receive an introduction to a justice system governed by process rather than outcome. This can be particularly important in cases where executive whim was substituted for respect for individual rights and the rule of law.[293]

National commissions or courts-martial can also serve important interests as well. First, they can provide a forum to try war criminals who were the action officers of the principals tried before an IMT. This can serve to relieve the pressure on the IMT while permitting the conduct of more trials within a reasonable proximity of the conduct in question. It can also serve as an important forum for prosecuting individual actors who have violated the laws of war for which the nation which convenes the commission has a palpable interest. For example, if the Iraqi guards that beat a downed American pilot in the Persian Gulf War could be identified, the United States would have a palpable interest in the guard's prosecution. But in a nation where horrific atrocities are a daily occurrence, it would fall below the appropriate jurisdiction of an international tribunal and be of little interest to domestic courts, if any existed, faced with identifying and prosecuting others of greater interest to the local

---

[293] For example, Iraq.

population. Such cases should be in the purview of the victim's nation and the prosecution should rest with them as such ends most serve the needs of justice for that nation especially when other effective forums are not available.

Further, to the extent possible and at the earliest point, the domestic courts need to be reestablished and made available to the domestic population for the prosecution of those who committed atrocities against them. It is important, however, that these courts be monitored in the transitional period to ensure that they are providing forums for justice and not vengeance. This is particularly important if the society is composed of diverse populations that have never integrated into a coherent society.

B. Domestic Reconciliation: Lessons Learned from South Africa?

Though "domestic reconciliation" by definition, the experience gained by the South Africans after the end of apartied can provide lessons learned that are beneficial to the role a post conflict system of justice can serve to aid in the ultimate reconciliation of the belligerents. After years of bloodshed and political upheaval culminating in the collapse of the apartied system of government, South Africa sought out as a matter of state policy to acknowledge that "many people are in need of healing, and we need to heal our country if we are to build a nation which will guarantee peace and stability."[294]

---

[294] JUSTICE IN TRANSITION, SOUTH AFRICA TRUTH AND RECONCILIATION COMMISSION (1995) (introduction by Dullah Omar), *available at* http://www.doj.gov.za/trc/legal/justice.htm.

The Truth and Reconciliation Commission was incorporated in the interim Constitution of South Africa. The Commission was part of a constitutional scheme to "[h]eal the divisions of the past and establish a society based on democratic values, social justice and fundamental human rights."[295] Further, the goal of the process included the strengthening of a democracy "committed to the building up of a human rights culture in our land."[296]

The Truth and Reconciliation Commission was in many respects a commission similar in nature to the Tribunals of World War II. While some of the activities, such as murder, that were within the purview of the commission were crimes under *domestic* law at the time of the offense, others were not. Much like the Nuremberg Tribunals that sought to punish those who committed crimes against humanity, the Truth and Reconciliation Commission set out to investigate "gross violations of human rights" and to be empowered to grant amnesty for "acts, omissions and offenses associated with political objectives committed in the course of the conflicts of the past."[297] The scope of the authority of the commission extended to acts committed by state actors presumably under the color of law.[298]

The South Africans viewed truth as the path to reconciliation of the belligerents. The price for amnesty was truth.[299] The focus was on the truth telling process as opposed to the

---

[295] S. AFR. CONST. (Constitution Act, 1993) ch. 1 (Preamble).

[296] JUSTICE IN TRANSITION, SOUTH AFRICA TRUTH AND RECONCILIATION COMMISSION (1995) (Introduction by Dullah Omar), *available at* http://www.doj.gov.za/trc/legal/justice.htm.

[297] Promotion of National Unity and Reconciliation Act (Act No. 34, July 26, 1995).

[298] JUSTICE IN TRANSITION, SOUTH AFRICA TRUTH AND RECONCILIATION COMMISSION (1995) (functions of the Commission), *available at* http://www.doj.gov.za/trc/legal/justice.htm.

[299] Promotion of National Unity and Reconciliation Act, sec. 16 (Act No. 34, July 26, 1995).

heinous nature of the crime for which amnesty was sought. For example, a security police

commander, Eugene de Kock, upon the submission of a petition for amnesty that was

deemed by the commission to be complete and truthful was granted full amnesty though his

crimes were marked by cold blooded brutality. De Kock admitted in his petition for amnesty

to his involvement in kidnapping four activists and taking them "to different secluded places

where each was killed and their bodies burned."[300] Others involved in the incident were not

as fortunate in their petitions that differed materially from that of de Kock.[301]

Though reconciliation is an important societal goal, the other traditional goals of the

criminal justice system serve important societal interests that cannot be ignored. The process

of punishment of the wrongdoer serves to varying degrees to bring closure to victims of

crime and their families. As truth served to bring amnesty from punishment to the

wrongdoer in the name of reconciliation, in South Africa procedures were developed to help

bring closure to the victims of crime, their families and their broader communities. Victims

in many cases became eligible for the payment of reparations from a government reparations

fund.[302] Further, the Committee on Reparation and Rehabilitation of Victims of the Truth

---

[300] *de Kock Granted Amnesty for Cradock Four Murders,* SOUTH AFRICAN PRESS ASSOCIATION (December 14, 1999) .

[301] *See id* and *TRC Refuses Amnesty to 9 Former Security Police,* SOUTH AFRICAN PRESS ASSOCIATION (December 13, 1999). Initially, de Kock was denied amnesty, but his version of the truth ultimately prevailed.

[302] SUMMARY OF REPARATION AND REHABILITATION POLICY, INCLUDING PROPOSALS TO BE CONSIDERED BY THE PRESIDENT, sec. 3 (undated), available at http://www.doj.gov.za/trc/reparations/summary.htm.

and Reconciliation Commission granted victims "an opportunity to relate their own accounts of the violations of which they are the victims . . . ."[303]

The lessons learned from the South African experience demonstrates that a truth and reconciliation process can serve to provide some degree of accountability while preparing a history of the events surrounding the atrocities. The process can also contribute to reconciliation. What is less clear, however, is the extent to which such a process should be available to the leaders of nations, the nation's key agents such as officers of state police and military organizations, and the population in general. If the process is not to be one of general application, what factors should be considered in deciding whether to grant amnesty in exchange for truthful participation?

The answer to this question will depend upon the nature of the conflict and the character of the violence undertaken. Other factors include whether it involved international armed conflict, and whether atrocities were primarily directed at discrete minorities as opposed to an environment in which the conduct had devolved to street violence among the various factions. Further, practical considerations such as the ability of domestic courts to process the volume of potential war criminals should also be considered.

In developing a post-conflict system of justice after the collapse or military defeat of a totalitarian regime with an extreme degree of centralized power, there are two classes of individuals who should be denied amnesty as a matter of policy. These classes of

---

[303] JUSTICE IN TRANSITION, SOUTH AFRICA TRUTH AND RECONCILIATION COMMISSION (1995) (Committee on Reparation and Rehabilitation of Victims), *available at* http://www.doj.gov.za/trc/legal/justice.htm.

perpetrators should be denied any form of amnesty as to do so could be construed as a ratification of their misconduct, while also damaging the reconciliation process by denying justice to the victims of the most brutal of criminals. Those ineligible should include first, any principals responsible for the purposeful use of weapons, conventional or otherwise, against civilian populations. Similarly, such an opportunity should be denied to those who direct illegal military operations against third party states or against minority or oppressed groups living within the borders of the country in question. Using Iraq as an example, the principal leaders of the nation responsible for directing, planning or executing invasions of countries such as Kuwait and Iran, and attacking the civilian populations of Israel and Saudi Arabia should be denied the opportunity to submit amnesty petitions.

The second category of individuals that should be denied the opportunity to petition a truth and reconciliation commission for amnesty are those who were responsible for direct participation in state sponsored or directed activities calculated to terrorize the population of the country or engage in violations of the law of war. For example, individuals involved in the use of rape and murder as tools for punishment and control of civilian dissidents should be ineligible. Likewise, those involved in the abuse of Allied POWs and similar misconduct should only be eligible for amnesty upon coordination and approval of the nation of the victim.[304]

As the British quickly deduced during its post-World War II experience in the Pacific, the justice system may not be able to handle all of the serious offenders identified after a conflict

---

[304] *See infra* notes 368-370 and accompanying text.

including elements of the classes identified above. In such cases, a consistent standard should be established for criminal conduct that would be eligible for amnesty as part of a truth and reconciliation process. This line, however, would be very fact specific and would be directly related to the capacity of the post-conflict justice system and the number of potential defendants.

When developing such a system, it is equally important to consider the impact that it will have on the domestic population. It must further the reconciliation of the domestic population and the restoration of peace. Accordingly, it must be accepted as an equitable system by the local population to be effective.

C. Modern Trend: Universal Jurisdiction as a Legalistic Threat to Future Stability

While truth and reconciliation commissions are by their nature conducted in close proximity to the area in which the crimes within their purview occurred, many modern trends in the prosecution of war criminals remove the court from its area of interest. This section will look at recent developments in international criminal practice and evaluate their effectiveness from the perspective of whether they serve the ultimate ends of post conflict stability and peace. Specifically this section will look at the increasing use of theories of universal jurisdiction to gain jurisdiction over perceived bad actors. The concept of universal jurisdiction has been expanded by some governments desiring to prosecute third party non-citizens living outside of their boundaries that they perceive as having violated international law. Modern trends toward this expansive concept of universal jurisdiction are disturbing in that the prosecutor need not be a member of a nation with a direct connection to the crime sought to be prosecuted. Thus, prosecutors attempting to exercise such jurisdiction will seek to utilize extradition treaties to affect process.[305]

Such creative efforts to bring those perceived as violating international law before a court with no physical connection to the country in which the crime occurred and no direct interest in the case itself sets the stage for destabilization. For example, assume country A has been involved in a war with country B. Further, assume that this conflict involved the commission of violations of the law of war by one or more of the parties involved. If a third party nation unrelated to the conflict attempted to, or was perceived to have the potential to exercise jurisdiction, it could facilitate the continuation of war. Under such circumstances, if country A's leader directed an aggressive war against country B, and the parties now want to cease hostilities, country A's leadership may have a disincentive to peace as there would be no effective method to negotiate amnesty from war crimes among the parties to the belligerency. Rather than being able to resolve the matter bilaterally, the offending nation may believe that continued hostilities are preferable to a peace in which other nations – including traditionally hostile ones – might attempt to bring allegations of war crimes after the cessation of hostilities.

Likewise, the recent attempts by third parties to seek the prosecution of General Augusto Pinochet sets a potentially destabilizing precedent. Pinochet, who gave up power in Chile peacefully after agreeing to return control to civilian authority through democratic elections,

---

[305] Henry A. Kissinger, *The Pitfalls of Universal Jurisdiction*, 80 FOR. AFF. 86, 86-88 (2001).

firmly held the reigns of power and there are some who consider him as a leader of his people in a fight against communism.[306] Future dictators who might consider leaving their regimes under international pressure may refrain from doing so for fear of prosecution by a third party with no direct interest in the matter at hand.

There was some speculation that prior to military action to topple his regime, Saddam Hussein might have chosen to go into exile as part of a proposal put forward by various gulf states to avert war.[307] Dictators such as Hussein need not look further than recent developments with Pinochet to see that it might be a better idea to have your forces fight to the last man than to be humiliated before the dock of some far off land that was not a party to the earlier discussions and with no direct interest in the outcome.

The same potential for instability can arise from reliance on a "cookie cutter" approach to international accountability through organs such as the International Criminal Court. Although Hussein, if alive, does not need to fear the exercise of jurisdiction over him as he did not launch operations into a territory of a contracting party of the Treaty of Rome, future tyrants will face decisions such as those discussed above. While some may argue that these systems deter the would-be tyrant from engaging in war crimes or crimes against humanity, it is noteworthy that the potential for prosecution for violations of international law did not deter Saddam Hussein. Such forums could very well deter or effectively prevent negotiations

---

[306] Nick Caistor, *Pinochet profile: Saviour or tyrant,* BBC NEWS, *at* http://www.news.bbc.co.uk/1/hi/special_report/1998/the_pinochet_file/198145.stm (July 9, 2001).

[307] David R. Sands, A*rab states voice support for Saddam's exile,* WASH. TIMES, *at* http://www.washtimes.com/world/20030104-24476360.htm (Jan. 4, 2003).

that provide varying degrees of amnesty in exchange for the prevention of war or the cessation of hostilities. As such, it is questionable whether such forums can effectively deter war.

Further, these schemes may work to prevent the cessation of hostilities, reconciliation and the restoration of peace. The reasons for this potentiality are similar to those related to the unilateral exercise of universal jurisdiction by a nation untouched by the conflict. Much as the ability of the United Nations Security Council to act is affected by its rotating membership, so can the judicial composition at a given point be expected to shape the nature of the prosecutions that are brought before it. Thus, dictators may choose to continue to wage war against their neighbors and subjugate their people because of the inability to select an exile option in the face of a potential prosecution before the ICC.

D. Modern Trend: The Special Court of Sierra Leone – Positive Prequel for the Future

Rather than rely on far away courts or other forms of universal jurisdiction, the United Nations opted to build upon existing domestic law in its development of a plan for post-conflict justice in Sierra Leone. The United Nations Security Council in Resolution 1315 explicitly recognized the role the domestic courts in upholding "international standards of justice, fairness and due process of law" can play in the "process of national reconciliation and to the restoration of peace."[308] This acknowledgment was backed up by a request to the

---

[308] S.C. Res. 1315, U.N. SCOR, 4186th mtg., U.N. Doc. S/RES/1315 (2000).

88

Secretary-General to "negotiate an agreement with the Government of Sierra Leone to create an independent special court."[309]

The Security Council further recommended the Special Court have broad jurisdiction for punishing "crimes against humanity, war crimes and other serious violations of international humanitarian law." Notably, the Security Council also recommended that the Special Court be provided with subject matter jurisdiction over activities that constituted "crimes under relevant Sierra Leonean law committed within the territory of Sierra Leone."[310] A process that not only serves to provide increased flexibility to the prosecutor in charging, but also serves to inject a local jurisprudential flavor into the process.

While the subject matter jurisdiction recommended by the Security Council was broad enough to recognize virtually every internationally and domestically recognized theory of culpability, the personal jurisdiction recommended by the Security Council was far more restrictive. The Security Council's recommendation was that personal jurisdiction attach "over persons who bear the greatest responsibility for the commission of the crimes [referenced herein]."[311]

Security Council Resolution 1315's guidance was implemented less than two years later with the consummation of an agreement between the United Nations and the Government of

---

[309] *Id.*

[310] *Id.*

[311] *Id.*

Sierra Leone "On the Establishment of a Special Court for Sierra Leone."[312] The stated

purpose of the Special Court echoed the personal jurisdiction recommended by the Security

Council: "to prosecute persons who bear the greatest responsibility for serious violations of

international humanitarian law and Sierra Leonean law . . . since 30 November 1996."[313]

The Agreement provided for the creation of both a self-contained trial court and an

appellate court.[314] The trial court is composed of three judges with one appointed by the

government of Sierra Leone and the other two selected by the United Nations Secretary-

General. Though the jurists appointed by the Secretary-General could be selected from any

country that submitted nominations, there was a stated preference for those nominees from

the region.[315]

This agreement was followed by the Statute for the Special Court for Sierra Leone that

laid out the procedural framework and subject matter jurisdiction of the Special Court.[316]

The court's personal jurisdiction was further refined to define the class of potential

defendants based upon the nature of their crimes. Specifically, the court had jurisdiction

over: those engaged in crimes against humanity as part of "a widespread or systematic attack

---

[312] Agreement Between the United Nations and the Government of Sierra Leone On the Establishment of a Special Court for Sierra Leone, Jan. 16, 2002, U.N.-Sierra Leone.

[313] *Id.* art. 1(1).

[314] *Id.* art. 2(1).

[315] Specifically, preference is given to member States of the Economic Community of West African States and the Commonwealth. . . ." *Id.* art. 2(2)(a).

[316] Statute of the Special Court for Sierra Leone, August 14, 2000, art. 12(1)(a), U.N. - S.L. at http://sierra.leone.com/org/specialcourtstatute.html [hereinafter Special Court Statute].

against any civilian population;"[317] acts committed or ordered by an individual which violate Common Article 3 of the Geneva Conventions and Additional Protocol II;[318] and persons who committed other serious violations of international law such as "directing attacks against the civilian population" or the conscription of children.[319] While the scope of these individual articles seem to expand the potential personal jurisdiction of the court broadly, Article 5 serves to restrict the body of Sierra Leonean law incorporated into the Special Court's jurisdiction.[320] The Special Court's subject matter jurisdiction based upon domestic law was restricted to crimes related to the abuse of young girls and the burning of some buildings.[321]

The enabling statute also reflected concern with maintaining the supremacy of the Special Court while permitting concurrent jurisdiction with the domestic courts. The statute reflected the following competing concerns: that accused should not have to stand trial before both the Special Court and domestic courts; that the domestic courts not serve as a means to shield criminal responsibility; and that certain truth and reconciliation procedures adopted by the

---

[317] *Id.* art. 2. The Article lists several examples of such acts to include murder, enslavement, deportation, rape and sexual slavery, political or racial based prosecutions, or any "[o]ther inhumane act[]." *Id.* art 2(a-i).

[318] *Id.* art. 3. This provided a broad source of potential jurisdiction which on its face appears to go beyond that envisioned by the Security Council essentially turning the court into a body with jurisdiction over any person that might commit a violation Common Article 3 regardless of the level of the perpetrator.

[319] *Id.* art. 4(a-c).

[320] The policy of the Prosecutor's Office is to avoid the use of this potential jurisdiction to the extent possible. The purpose for this avoidance is to avoid possible challenges to the exercise of such jurisdiction under legal theories based upon Sierra Leonean law. Interview with David Crane, Chief Prosecutor, Special Court of Sierra Leone (February 13, 2003) (interview notes on file with the author).

[321] Special Court Statute, *supra* note 316, art. 5(a-b) (2002).

government of Sierra Leone could not be used to grant amnesty to those who committed crimes against humanity or "other serious violations of international law."

To prevent the possibility of the accused standing trial before two forums, the statute includes a *non bis in idem* clause.[322] This clause blocks all subsequent prosecution by a domestic court for offenses tried before the Special Court. It also greatly restricts the circumstances in which the Special Court could exercise jurisdiction after a domestic prosecution for a crime within the Special Court's jurisdiction. The Special Court could only pursue such a prosecution on evidence that the domestic court was not "impartial," or that the domestic prosecution was a sham.[323]

The statute also reflects the concern that amnesty granted by a domestic truth and reconciliation commission could frustrate the purposes of the Special Court. Accordingly, the statute prohibits the effective use of amnesty by domestic bodies when the crimes fall within the broad categories of activities described in Articles 2 and 4. The interaction of these two provisions provides an incomplete "fix" as the plain meaning of Article 2 seems to capture every individual actor caught up in the chaos that was Sierra Leone. It is difficult to envision the effective use of a truth and reconciliation procedure that did not have the authority to grant honest participants immunity from prosecution.

---

[322] *Id.* art. 9.

[323] *Id.* art. 9(2)(b).

As such, in theory this possibility serves to greatly limit the potential effectiveness of the truth and reconciliation commission to process those that could become the target of a Special Court prosecution, but in practice may not. This concern is minimized by practical approaches to the problem undertaken by the Chief Prosecutor David Crane. One such factor that serves to minimize a potential disconnect is that Mr. Crane views the Special Court as a forum for major criminals on the scale of those prosecuted before the IMT Nuremberg.[324] Nonetheless, many who could fall within the technical jurisdiction of the Special Court might reasonably be expected to refrain from appearing before a truth and reconciliation commission based upon generalized statements of its Chief Prosecutor.

The Special Court forged in Sierra Leone is a great modern model to consider when formulating a plan for a system of post-conflict justice, and as the work of the court continues so will the lessons learned. And though it is not the only modern *ad hoc* tribunal approaching the problem of meeting the ends of justice in a war torn society, it appears to be the model currently in use that has the greatest likelihood of success.[325] The strengths of the court as well as its weaknesses provide important guidance along side the lessons learned from post World War II prosecutions. These lessons can be applied to the problem of justice and accountability in the future, such as in post-conflict Iraq.

VI. Retooling the Past: A new dock for modern war criminals

---

[324] Jess Bravin, *Tribunal in Africa May Serve as Model for Trial of Hussein*, WSJ, Feb. 12, 2003, at B1.

[325] *See, e.g.*, Peter Ford, *Serbs still ignore role in atrocity*, THE CHRISTIAN SCI. MONITOR (Feb. 11 2002), *available at* http://www.csmonitor.com/2002/0211/p01s02-woeu.html.

No to war? What about no to tyranny?[326]

When developing a system for the prosecution of war criminals in a post-conflict Iraq, much can be learned from the international communities experience in the major theaters of operation after World War II, as well as from more recent undertakings such as those seen in South Africa and Sierra Leone. And as Iraq has not signed the Statute of Rome, the courts that prosecute the Iraqi war criminals will be *ad hoc* in nature. The greatest strength of *ad hoc* forums, however, is their ability to adapt their procedures to changing circumstances while upholding a consistent approach to what is considered criminal. As such, *ad hoc* tribunals and commissions must learn from the past while not becoming a slave to it. The problem in Iraq is similar in many respects to that faced in Japan, but different in many key respects. In developing an appropriate system, consideration must be given to the cultural, ethnic and religious landscape of Iraq.

A. Iraq's Multicultural Face

Iraq is a multicultural society composed of a collection of diverse ethnic and religious groups. These groups include the Kurds, Shiite Arabs, Sunni Arabs, Turkmen, Assyrians, Yazidis, Jews and Christians.[327] Many of these people were forcibly displaced by the Iraqi regime, to include the Shi'i Arabs, Kurds, Turkmen and the Assyrians.[328] As such, Iraq has

---

[326] Barham A. Salih, *Give Us a Chance to Build a Democratic Iraq*, N.Y. TIMES, Feb. 5. 2003, at A31. Barham A. Salih is the Co-Prime Minister of the Kurdistan Regional Government, Iraq.

[327] *Id.*

[328] *Secretary General's Representative on Internal Displacement visits Turkey*, GLOBAL IDP WEEKLY NEWS (June 12, 2002), *at* http://www.idpproject.org/weekly_news/2002/weekly_news_june02_2.htm.

the largest number of displaced people of any country in the middle east with totals potentially as high as one million.[329] The diversity and size of these displaced populations will need to be considered during all phases of reconstruction in Iraq to ensure that all populations share in the potential arising from the country's liberation from Saddam Hussein.

These groups have fared differently during the last few years under Saddam Hussein. The Kurds in the northern areas of Iraq have benefited under the protection of Allied fighters patrolling the Northern no-fly zones. Out from under the yoke of the official Iraqi regime, the Kurds "plant[ed] the seeds of democracy in soil that has for too long been given over to tyranny."[330] Further, this embryonic oasis of freedom is, like Iraq, a multicultural area with many ethnic minorities living voluntarily in the area controlled by the Kurdistan Regional Government.[331]

These minorities have elected to live in a developing democracy under the protection of Allied war planes rather than live under the former tyranny of Saddam Hussein. This Kurdish microcosm has faced its own difficult internal problems, but the experience of the Kurds demonstrates that peace and democracy can take hold in the region when the conditions are right.

---

[329] *Id.*

[330] Barham A. Salih, *Give Us a Chance to Build a Democratic Iraq*, N.Y. TIMES, Feb. 5. 2003, at A31.

[331] In addition to the beginnings of representative democracy in Kurdistan, they also enjoy a press "with hundreds of newspapers, magazines and television stations." *Id.*

Iraq's motives for the displacement of the Kurds and other ethnic minorities flow from a complicated mix of political and financial reasons. On one level, Iraq's mass murder and deportation of Kurds was part of Hussein's pan-Arab nationalistic movement towards the Arabization of Iraq. These actions by the former Iraqi government have been described as "genocidal" by Human Rights Watch, and over the last twenty years have resulted in the destruction of thousands of Kurdish areas and the displacement of hundreds of thousands of Kurds.[332]

On another level, the actions of Iraq have served to remove the Kurds and other non-Arabs from oil rich areas near Kirkuk. Though these populations were often given the opportunity to "correct" their nationality to Arab, those unwilling to convert were subjected to various forms of harassment to include arrest and forced relocation.[333] To add to this instability, Iraq relocated Arab Shi'a populations from the south to Kirkuk to frustrate Kurdish claims to land in the area and "to affirm the 'Arabic' character of the city."[334]

Though ostensibly these relocations of Shi'a Arabs to the north were part of the Arabization program, they were more a function of Hussein's desire to crush his Shiite opponents to the South.[335] These groups who engaged in an unsuccessful uprising after the

---

[332] *Secretary General's Representative on Internal Displacement visits Turkey*, GLOBAL IDP WKLY NEWS (June 12, 2002), *at* http://www.idpproject.org/weekly_news/2002/weekly_news_june02_2.htm.

[333] *Id.*

[334] *Id.*

[335] This includes both the Marsh Arabs and the broader Shi'a communities in the south. Many of the Shi'a leaders were perceived as a threat by Saddam Hussein and were eliminated. JOHN FAWCETT & VICTOR TANNER, THE INTERNALLY DISPLACED PEOPLE OF IRAQ 28 (The Brookings Institution-SAIS Project on Internal Displacement 2002).

Persian Gulf War became a source of concern to the Iraqi regime. Further, many of these individuals lived in a marshland that provided a great deal of protection from land attack and benefited from the southern no-fly zone. This marshland was destroyed, however, by Saddam Hussein to starve out the Shiites and thus force their relocations to points north or out of Iraq.[336]

Thus a 5,000 year old Marsh Arab culture and homeland was destroyed to further Hussein's political aims. Before doing so, however, the Iraqi government launched a massive propaganda campaign to reinforce and amplify traditional Iraqi views of these Marsh Arabs as backward "monkey-faced people" who "were not real Iraqis."[337] These efforts not only resulted in a massive environmental catastrophe, but also served to legitimize and maximize Sunni hatred of the Shi'a Marsh Arabs. Iraq's efforts to institutionalize hatred for this minority will further complicate the post-Saddam Hussein Iraq.

Assyrians also suffered under Saddam Hussein. The Assyrians are predominantly Christian and until the 1970s lived in the area now occupied by the Kurdish Regional Government. After the destruction of 200 of their villages by the Iraqi government, they

---

[336] Hussein accomplished this by building a series of dams to divert water away from the marshland. This plan to force the relocation of these Shi'a Arabs resulted in the destruction of the largest marshland in Iraq. *Secretary General's Representative on Internal Displacement visits Turkey*, GLOBAL IDP WKLY NEWS (June 12, 2002), *at* http://www.idpproject.org/weekly_news/2002/weekly_news_june02_2.htm.

[337] JOHN FAWCETT & VICTOR TANNER, THE INTERNALLY DISPLACED PEOPLE OF IRAQ 29 (The Brookings Institution-SAIS Project on Internal Displacement 2002).

were relocated south to the city of Baghdad.[338] Since the Persian Gulf War, the Assyrians also claim that they have been further displaced by the Kurds.[339]

Prior to the termination of his regime by military action, Saddam Hussein created a difficult situation for the world community that must now struggle with the myriad of issues he has left behind as his legacy. With the termination of his regime, the stage is set for civil war as the various displaced groups seek to reclaim areas which they view as their own. In the North, land could become subject to simultaneous claims by Kurds, Turkmen, Assyrians, Shi'a, Sunni Arabs and others.[340] Thus, it is now critical for the international community to develop institutions in Iraq that will serve to centralize control in the near term, while setting the stage for a peaceful transition to a new Iraqi government at the earliest opportunity.

In addition to the complexity and potential for hostility injected into Iraq by Hussein's active policies of displacement, the complicated religious landscape will also be a matter of concern. Iraq is composed of large populations of Sunni and Shi'a Muslims and significant populations of Christians and Jews. It is therefore critical that Iraq be placed squarely on a path toward a secular government that can meet the needs of this multicultural society.[341]

---

[338] *Id.* at 14.

[339] *Id.*

[340] *Id.* at 24-5. The Brookings Institute Report recommends that restitution be paid to those who have been disposed of their property and that the these forced dislocations be recognized and prosecuted by the international community. *Id.* at 48-9.

[341] This is one of the greatest challenges facing not only a post-conflict Iraq, but modernization efforts throughout the middle east. The use of shariah law derived directly from the Quran as opposed to law codified by a legislative or government body would serve to create the foundations of an Islamic state. In the words of one prominent scholar: "An Islamic state is necessarily a theocracy." RAM SWARUP, UNDERSTANDING THE HADITH: THE SACRED TRADITIONS OF ISLAM 124 (Prometheus Books Edition 2002).

Further, such a path will prevent the rise of a theocracy with the inherent potential to oppress those outside of its faith. In keeping with this concern, all levels of courts that are established in the wake of Saddam Hussein should be of a secular nature.

This is not to suggest that the society that congeals in Iraq cannot borrow from the traditions of Islam and other religions. However, the courts available to the citizens of Iraq cannot be different for the various races, sects and genders. Accordingly, the source of law must ultimately flow from a legislative body open to representatives of the various populations of Iraq. Religious courts by their nature often discriminate against non-believers and others. As one Muslim scholar notes:

> An Islamic state is totalitarian in the philosophic sense. A closed politics or civics is a necessary corollary of a closed theology. In Islam, the concept of *ummah* dominates over the concept of man or mankind. So in a Muslim polity, only Muslims have full political rights in any sense of the term; non-Muslims, if they are allowed to exist at all as a result of various exigencies, are *zimmis*, second-class citizens.[342]

The development of a system of post-conflict justice in Iraq should rely in part upon domestic courts and traditions. However, efforts must be undertaken to resist and prevent the development of domestic theocratic courts that could become the vehicle of tyranny for believers and non-believers alike. The development of domestic courts can pull from the traditions of all of the nations within Iraq to include the Sunni and Shi'a legal traditions. These traditions have a rich history of scholarship related to the concept of justice. This includes scholarly recognition that the "more advanced the[] procedural rules, the higher []

---

[342] *Id.* at 124-5.

99

the quality of formal justice revealed in that particular system of law."[343] The task for those

reconstructing Iraq will be to ensure that the legal system treats *all* equally before it rather

than allow the system to adopt the narrow view that "Law is to protect the interests of

believers as a whole . . . ."[344]

B. Borrowing from the Past & Present – Justice in Post-Conflict Iraq

The brief discussion above of the complexities surrounding the ethnic and religious

landscape of modern Iraq represents only a superficial sketch of the problems that will face

those tasked with the awesome responsibility of reconstructing a society that has been

plagued by decades of tyranny and war. It reveals, however, the need for the international

community to remain heavily engaged in the development and execution of systems of

justice to punish those responsible for bringing war and terror on generations of those living

in and near Iraq. The courts must be courts of justice not tools of vengeance. They must in

the end contribute to the reconciliation of this war torn society and the foundations of a future

peace. Any component of a system that does not further these goals should be rejected

during the period of reconstruction.

The lessons from World War II and those that continue to be learned from progressive

forums such as the Special Court of Sierra Leone provide a wealth of information for

---

[343] MAJID KHADDURI, THE ISLAMIC CONCEPTION OF JUSTICE 136 (Johns Hopkins Press 1984). This is an excellent text on the development of the various schools of thought on what constitutes justice under Islamic Law.

[344] *Id.* at 138.

planners today. These lessons reveal that a system that leverages the resources of the international community, to include national commissions operating within an established framework, and those of the domestic courts of the fallen nation can best serve the interests of justice and peace. Such a multi-tiered system of justice serves to permit the establishment of an International Tribunal that can focus solely on the thirty or forty top principals of Iraq.[345] Lesser international criminals can then be prosecuted by other national commissions constituted under the auspices of a Control Council similar to that established by the international community in Germany after World War II. Domestic courts could further augment this system. Those whose criminality falls below the level of conduct that the post-conflict system can reasonably accommodate could be considered for processing by a truth and reconciliation commission.

Thus, international justice in Iraq should be meted out from several levels. These levels are: an International Military Tribunal; a broad collection of national commissions reflecting nations who have a palpable interest[346] in the prosecution of Iraqi war criminals; domestic criminal courts to handle matters of isolated violence against individuals; and domestic civil courts to direct the investigation of claims of government action related to abusive policies. Lastly, the Iraqi people should with the assistance of the international community establish a truth and reconciliation commission to serve as an alternative to prosecution for the many

---

[345] Currently, the Bush administration publicly identified twelve individuals who could be tried for war crimes by an international tribunal after the liberation of Iraq. These individuals include President Saddam Hussein, his sons and top supporters such as Ali "Chemical Ali" Hassan al-Majid. *See* Barry Schweid, *Bush lists Iraqi war-crimes suspects*, WASH. TIMES (Mar. 17, 2003), *at* http://www.washtimes.com/world/20030317-81288520.htm

[346] "Palpable interest" is used to mean interests that touch on the nation's sovereignty such as seeking justice for the victimization of its citizens by the offending nation.

individual acts of violence that will come to light that undoubtedly have touched all of the nations within Iraq. This system should be implemented under the oversight of a Control Council whose charter would ideally be sanctioned by the United Nations Security Council. This proposed system is discussed in greater detail below and is depicted graphically at the attached appendix.

This system would also serve as a framework on which to graft military commissions operating as occupation courts.[347] The Tribunals and commissions in forms discussed above, however, would be concerned with criminal conduct that occurred prior to the date of the cessation of hostilities, while occupation courts would be concerned with a far broader range of criminal behavior that occurred after the liberation of Iraq. Over time the instrumentalities of these systems would collapse into the Iraqi domestic courts as Iraq slowly returns to a civil society capable of self-governance. As such, the domestic courts as they are strengthened will serve as an important bridge from liberation to self-reliance.

This approach will leverage the lessons of the past, and is also consistent with the goals of democratization and the establishment of the rule of law. In the words of President George W. Bush in describing his goals for American foreign policy: "We will defend the peace by fighting terrorists and tyrants. We will preserve the peace by building good relations among the great powers. We will extend the peace by encouraging free and open

---

[347] The operation of the "occupation courts" is beyond the scope of this work, but should be brought ultimately under the control of the proposed Control Council.

societies on every continent."[348] With these goals in mind, the President hopes to give the various developing countries the power to "choose for themselves the rewards and challenges of political and economic freedom."[349] This proposal contributes to the attainment of these goals by providing a framework for the prosecution of war criminals, alongside other reconstruction efforts, that can help place the possibility of a lasting peace in the hands of the citizens of Iraq.

1. The International Military Tribunal – Iraq

The model for an International Military Tribunal for Iraq should resemble the approach the Allies used in post-war Japan as opposed to that of the IMT at Nuremberg with inspiration for developing close relations ultimately with domestic institutions as forged by Sierra Leone's Special Court. The Japanese model reflected a broad constituency of the victors and representatives of nations that had been victimized by the Japanese. Such a Tribunal is well-suited for the trial of major war criminals in Iraq.

The development of an IMT for Iraq should consider the inclusion of several constituencies. Broadly, these constituencies should include representatives from the nations who provided the military might necessary to remove Hussein's regime, representatives of nations that were victimized by Iraq, and representatives of the broader international

---

[348] THE NATIONAL SECURITY STRATEGY OF THE UNITED STATES OF AMERICA (Sept. 2002) (introductory comments by President Bush).

[349] Id.

103

community. The developers of the Court could also consider the inclusion of a representative of the Iraqi people.

At present, the United States, the United Kingdom and Australia would be leading contenders for sending representatives to the Tribunal because of their service in removing the regime and their natural interest in ensuring that the subsequent legal actions be conducted in a manner consistent with international due process norms. The nations that have been victimized by Saddam Hussein include Kuwait, Israel, Saudi Arabia and Iran. As such, these nations should also be considered as sources of jurists to sit in judgment of any captured survivors of Saddam Hussein and his crew.[350] Lastly, the representative of the Iraqi people should not necessarily be from a dissident group or a displaced people. The horrors that will be revealed by such a tribunal will not require the potentially jaundiced eye of a dissident leader to decipher. The greatest legitimacy will be added if an Iraqi jurist can be identified from outside of Saddam Hussein's Ba'thist party, but who has managed to avoid direct victimization by the regime itself.

The final rules and procedures to govern the Tribunal should be developed under the direction of the jurists selected for service on the tribunal. These jurists should be given broad latitude to develop procedural and evidentiary standards for the tribunal. This latitude

---

[350] Integrating Persians, Sunni and Shi'a Arabs, westerners and Israelis into a post-conflict judicial system may be a political and cultural "bridge too far." But the concept as daunting as it is should be studied. Part of a plan of a broader peace in the Middle East necessitates that nations surrounding Iraq recognize the right of each other to exist. Though far beyond the scope of this paper, requiring the various parties to recognize the legitimacy of one another in their actions could help further develop a platform for a lasting peace. This is a particularly important consideration in light of recent efforts by the Bush Administration to craft a lasting regional peace for the region. *See, e.g.*, Guy Dinmore & Harvey Morris, *Powell foresees tough going ahead with road map*, FIN. TIMES, May 10, 2003, at 3.

should not be without limits, however. The standards should be required to be developed consistent with international norms as manifest and reflected in the Charter of the Tribunal as developed by the international community and under the daily control of a Control Council.[351] The final rules of the Tribunal should be subject to approval from the Control Council. Such required approval will alleviate the need to permit appeals based upon any theory that the Rules promulgated by the Tribunal were inconsistent with the direction or limitations developed by the Control Council.

The Tribunal will enjoy the greatest degree of legitimacy among the Iraqis as well as with the broader international community if the jurists are permitted to develop the rules and procedures that will govern the International Tribunal subject to the limitations imposed upon it by the Control Council.[352] Such an arrangement will serve two potentially conflicting goals: respect for due process of law and the assimilation of key legal systems to further the legitimacy of the Tribunal.

First, through the auspices of the United Nations and the Iraqi Control Council, it will be possible to ensure that the Tribunal and other courts and commissions responsible for prosecuting international criminals maintain the due process standards required by modern notions of fundamental fairness. Second, it will serve to force moderation within the

---

[351] *See infra* notes 371-381 and accompanying text.

[352] The scope of the representation would be based upon practical considerations such as how many jurists could sit effectively. The IMT was composed of four, but the IMTFE was composed of eleven. Regardless, there should be no more than one member permitted from any particular country. The Office of the Chief Prosecutor would also be an appropriate forum for broad multi-national representation as was the case in both theaters after World War II.

Tribunal itself by the process of reconciling jurists trained under Common, Civil, and Islamic legal traditions. Though these traditions vary, the experience of World War II demonstrates that these differences can be harmonized especially when developed under the ultimate auspices of a higher control council. Further, though the Tribunal must be secular, it can nonetheless draw from the Islamic legal tradition.[353] For example, Islamic scholars have long recognized that it was criminal to wage an unjust war "motivated by the Ruler's personal . . . lust for power, honor or glory" or "wars of conquest waged by the Ruler for the subordination of people other than the people of the city over which he presides."[354] These notions nest well with western notions of the crime of aggression, for example.

The Office of the Chief Prosecutor before the International Military Tribunal for Iraq should be organized in a similar manner. At a minimum, prosecutors should represent the nations who have been selected to represent the world community on the Tribunal itself. The prosecutor's office, however, provides greater opportunity for representation of country's with a direct interest in the prosecution of key Iraqi war criminals.

As with the opportunity provided to the Tribunal for the development of its own rules, a multinational approach to the development of indictments against the major Iraqi war criminals will serve to ensure a conservative approach to charging and thus yield the greatest

---

[353] The Tribunal should not be purely shaped in an Islamic tradition, however. Like the Tribunals after World War II, it can take on procedures that reflect the harmonization of several systems of law to render justice before a multinational body. *See supra* notes 150-172 and accompanying text.

[354] KHADDURI, *supra* note 343, at 172. Note that under Shari'a law wars against other peoples was considered just if conducted for the purpose of killing those who refused to convert to Islam after being offered the opportunity. *Id.* Thus the need to divorce the court from any ties to a specific religion to ensure legitimacy.

resulting domestic and international legitimacy. Ideally, prosecutors should strive to develop charges that are agreeable to all of the parties involved to maximize the perception of fairness surrounding the indictment. All national representatives should be required to concur or non-concur by endorsement with the final indictments.[355]

The development of the rules governing the Tribunals and the indictments will take time.[356] History has taught, however, that these important undertakings must be pursued methodically with less concern for efficiency than the perceptions that the Tribunal will create in the minds of the domestic population and the world.[357] With the eyes of the world on the process, "efficient" processing will harm the overall interests of justice in the developing world. The execution of a just process with due regard for the rights of the subject carefully weighed against the need for appropriate evidentiary standards tailored to the exigencies of the circumstances will serve to strengthen the respect for the rule of law in transitional societies. Society's need to bring justice to key members of Saddam Hussein's former regime must also be considered.

---

[355] The ratio of concurrences to non-concurrences necessary to go forward on a prosecution is a political decision. However, the greater the number, especially with respect to the theory of criminality, the greater the legitimacy that the process brings to the court. Prosecutors should strive to reach 100 percent concurrence even if the rules established do not require it.

[356] It will also take a significant amount of time to properly investigate the atrocities committed or directed by the major international criminals. Procedural rules can be developed while the Control Council directs the investigation of these crimes. In light of the breadth of atrocities committed under the Hussein regime, it is quite possible that the Tribunal could be prepared to begin its work before the investigators are completed with theirs.

[357] Planners should strive to avoid what is perceived broadly as a rush to justice as has been the case with *In re Yamashita*, 66 S. Ct. 340, 363 n. 9 (1946). *See supra* notes 234-237 and accompanying text.

The proceedings of the Tribunal should be broadly disseminated and public viewing should be encouraged. Transparency of its actions will help legitimize its work in the eyes of the Iraqi people, the Middle Eastern community and the world. Televised broadcasts distributed worldwide via the Internet and satellite should be given due consideration to educate the world on the horrors visited upon Iraq.[358] Further, such wide dissemination will aid in the reduction of conspiracy theories and other rhetorical attacks on the work of the Tribunal that might be perpetrated by individuals or groups that have an interest in preventing the democratization of countries within the greater Middle East.[359] An International Military Tribunal for Iraq will serve the ultimate goals of peace and reconciliation, but in order to meet these higher goals it is critical that the proceedings be available to all who stand to benefit from the democratization of the region.

2. National Military Commissions

---

[358] The author generally does not support the broadcast of domestic court proceedings, but the broadcast of trials of such international concern will provide a rare opportunity to both educate the world as to the actions of Hussein's Iraq while also exposing the populations of other nations to the judicial institutions of modern democracies. The importance of such a process was foreshadowed by a comment in that appeared in the *Frankfurter Allgemeine Zeitung* after Secretary of State Colin Powell made his case against Iraq before the UN Security Council. This German paper noted: "The performance was undeniably brilliant. In doing so, the American secretary of state turned the Security Council into a kind of world court; he himself played the role of prosecution. What was so impressive in the evidence was . . . its breadth." *Powell's Performance Earns Mixed Reviews*, N.Y. TIMES, Feb. 7, 2003, at A10 (quoting the FRANKFURTER ALLEGEMEINE ZEITUNG) (no point source indicated).

[359] There will need to be provisions for safeguarding classified information, although it is not clear to what degree such information, even if available, would be necessary to obtain a conviction of Saddam Hussein and his close associates.

Nations with a palpable interest in crimes committed by Iraqi officials and agents should be permitted to establish national commissions within the borders of Iraq.[360] Such a palpable interest could flow from nations whose POWs were tortured or subjected to unlawful acts of aggression by the Iraqi regime. Further, as with the commissions conducted by nations in Germany after World War II, they should take on an international character[361] by being subordinated to an international control council.[362] These commissions though governed to a great extent by local regulation promulgated by the nation involved, should be required to comply with certain minimum standards established by the multinational Control Council.

This international coordinating body can be used to ensure that the procedures adopted by national commissions meet minimum procedural and evidentiary requirements while ensuring that the burdens of proof are consistent with criminal prosecutions. At a minimum these regulations could be used to ensure that all national commission ensure access to counsel and the ability to prepare a defense, that evidentiary standards apply equally to the prosecution and the defense, and that prosecutors be required to prove their case beyond a reasonable doubt to obtain a conviction. Such a control council could also define the scope of the jurisdiction of the national courts.

---

[360] Nations should also be permitted to seek extradition of suspected Iraqi war criminals for act contrary to the domestic laws of various nations. For example, if evidence were developed that demonstrated that a particular Iraqi had been involved in terrorist activities directed at the United States in violation of United States domestic law, petitions for extradition should be permitted. Before extradition, however, the accused should first be tried before the appropriate international forum if the international community desires such prosecution.

[361] Nations conducting commissions in Germany after World War II considered them to have an international character that superceded their national character because of their creation under the auspices of the international Control Council. *See Rules and Practice Concerning Various Types of Evidence, supra* note 203, at 627, 627.

[362] For a discussion of how a proposed control council could operate in Iraq, *see infra* notes 371-381 and accompanying text.

Further, to ensure compliance with the minimum international norms established by the Control Council regulations, all appeals should made directly to a multinational appeals chamber as opposed to the appellate courts of the various nations involved. These appeals should be limited to the legal requirements specifically required by the Control Council regulations and to ensure factual sufficiency to support the underlying convictions. Convictions should receive final approval by the Control Council itself.

3. Domestic Courts

Reconstruction efforts in Iraq should quickly focus on the redevelopment of the Iraqi domestic courts as part of broader efforts toward democratization. These courts should be built upon the existing structure of the domestic courts while ensuring that necessary reforms are introduced to ensure compliance with fundamental norms. Further, these courts should be relied upon to the greatest extent possible for prosecuting those who commit atrocities that fall below the jurisdiction of the International Military Tribunal or the interest of the national commissions.

During the reconstruction phase, however, it will be critical that the international community ensure that the domestic justice system not be "captured" by one particular sect or ethnic group. Further, these courts must be reconstituted as secular courts as opposed to religious tribunals. This is critical to ensuring that there are no perceptions that the domestic courts are instruments of any particular group.

The domestic courts should also be involved in the investigation and resolution of claims related to Iraq's Arabization program.[363] As this program has in effect created multiple levels of claims with varying degrees of legitimacy to the same property, it will require a complicated investigatory process that may reveal more than one individual who has developed interests in property through no misconduct of their own. A domestic court or investigative body would be in the best position to investigate and evaluate these claims. Unfortunately, such a body also has the greatest likelihood to be "captured" by a particular faction and turned into a system of distributing spoils. Accordingly, this aspect of the domestic system will need to be closely scrutinized by the international community.[364]

Further, as domestic courts begin functioning, they should be encouraged to investigate and prosecute Iraqis who violated domestic and international law within their borders. In addition, these courts should be given independent charging authority as soon as practicable. However, such authority should be coordinated with the Control Council if the domestic courts desire that their actions to be final actions without the possibility of additional legal jeopardy. Thus, a framework should be established whereby the domestic courts request the release of primary jurisdiction from the international control council to the local court

---

[363] Initially, this program should be under the direct management of the Control Council with the members of the various investigative bodies drawn from the various populations within Iraq. As the domestic courts become functional and are in the position to take on some of the responsibility, they should be utilized to resolve disputes to the extent possible. Events that have transpired in the early days of post-Hussein Iraq, however, demonstrate the importance for a methodical and well reasoned transfer of authority over to Iraqi courts. One of many examples of the level of hostilities that devide Iraqis along cultural and political lines is a recent declaration that Shia Muslims should kill Ba'athists that may attempt to come out of hiding. James Drummond & Nicolas Pelham, *Shia clerics urge faithful to attack returning Ba'athists*, FIN. TIMES, May 10, 2003, at 3.

[364] For an excellent work on this and other issues that will face those tasked with rebuilding Iraq, *see* JOHN FAWCETT & VICTOR TANNER, THE INTERNALLY DISPLACED PEOPLE OF IRAQ 48-51 (The Brookings Institution-SAIS Project on Internal Displacement 2002).

regardless of who holds the defendant. This will aid in the resolution in competing requests for jurisdiction while serving to permit the termination of international jurisdiction over the person and thus the possibility for duplicative trials. Once jurisdiction is released by the Control Council, other courts forums operating under the auspices of the Control Council would be divested of jurisdiction. Learning from concepts developed for use in Sierra Leone, this divestiture could only be overcome if the Control Council subsequently determined that the prosecution carried out by the domestic court was conducted in a manner designed to shield the perpetrator from punishment.

Further, by providing international oversight of the reestablishing domestic courts, it helps to ensure that the local forums will be able to develop gradually without becoming overwhelmed. It also minimizes the likelihood that the courts will be permitted independently until such point that it has been established that they can function in a manner consistent with the rule of law. As such, the international community acting through the Control Council should make the determination as to the extent and timing of the independence of the post-conflict Iraqi domestic courts.

4. Truth and Reconciliation Commission

The history of modern war has brought with it the desire to bring justice to those who commit grave breaches of international law. It has also brought the recognition that the extreme volume of potential defendants can overwhelm any traditional system of justice. At best, this provides the basis for subsequent claims that the system was inequitable for prosecuting some, while thousands who committed similar or more egregious offenses were ultimately set free. At worst, it gives rise to a system that could resemble collective vengeance more than a quest for justice.

This concern is not new. For example, the British in the Pacific theater during World War II faced the problem of the sheer magnitude of those who had been actively involved in war crimes especially with respect to the maltreatment of POWs. The British command in the Pacific was concerned that if they did not consider the massive number of defendants in organizing their commissions, they would ultimately be accused of inconsistency in prosecution or, perhaps worse, simply using the commissions as a tool to further humiliate a vanquished people. To combat this, any war criminals that were determined likely to receive less than seven years from a military commission were effectively given amnesty.[365]

The problem with this approach is that it fails to provide any closure or accountability in cases that do not meet the established criteria. This void can be filled using a truth and reconciliation commission that builds upon the lessons learned in Sierra Leone.[366] The combined result offers a pragmatic system for justice that also facilitates closure for those involved thus providing the best possibility for future peace and reconciliation. And like the

---

[365] *See supra* notes 268-269 and accompanying text.

[366] *See supra* notes 322-324 and accompanying text.

British in World War II, it should establish a threshold standard below which petitions for amnesty will be considered by the commission.[367]

Such a commission should be domestic in character with broad representation by the various ethnic groups and religious sects within Iraq.[368] Further, the process for obtaining amnesty should rest with the individual, not with the commission itself. Individuals who believe that they may be entitled to such an amnesty should be required to provide a detailed description of their misconduct to include the names of any known victims and surviving family members. Their petition should include a statement that they are willing to provide further truthful testimony to the commission if necessary as requested and cooperate with any lawfully constituted court, commission or tribunal operating under the auspices of the international community or domestic authority. There should be a very limited period during which individuals are given the opportunity to file such requests.

The initial review of the petition should be by the members of the commission itself. If the commission determines that the petition appears to meet the requirements for amnesty, they will forward it to the Control Council for ultimate approval.[369] This process will ensure

---

[367] "Major war criminals" over which the International Military Tribunal for Iraq should not be able to perfect amnesty through this process, not should individuals of significant concern to a particular concern to the international community that might be a candidate for prosecution before a military commission.

[368] Initially, such a body may need to be under the direct management and control of the Control Council. Nonetheless, it should be primarily composed of Iraqis from various groups and backgrounds.

[369] It is not pragmatically possible to propose a viable list of proposed requirements without evaluating the situation on the ground after the liberation of Iraq. The criteria should be such that they permit amnesty for a consistent list of misconduct that facilitates consistency in outcome and legitimacy in the process. It will be crucial that the system developed not be perceived as favoring one ethnic or minority group in Iraq over another.

that an organ of the domestic government will not be in the position to grant a general amnesty to a person wanted by the broader international community. It will also ensure that individuals do not subject themselves to a process believing that they have obtained immunity from the various international forums in Iraq when in fact they have not.

When the Control Council reviews an amnesty petition, it should be staffed through the various offices of the International Military Tribunal as well as the representatives of the various nations that may have an interest in the matter. This process will also facilitate the prosecution of other war criminals, as the petitioners may be a source of direct testimony against other subjects further up the chain of command. As such, the window of opportunity for suspects to petition the commission should be aligned to the extent possible with the main war crimes investigative phase. After such multilateral coordination, the Control Council should either reject the petition, or return it to the domestic authorities for final action. If at such time amnesty is granted, it would serve to divest any forum operating under the auspices of the Control Council from jurisdiction over the matter.

This process will aid in the restoration of peace while providing accountability for wrongs committed. The integration of a truth and reconciliation component in to a post-conflict system of justice will require the coordination of many domestic and international governmental and non-governmental organizations. This is the role of a Control Council located on the ground in Iraq. The maximization of the use of judicial processes within the territory of Iraq is crucial to success. Keeping the instruments of justice close to the affected

population will maximize their exposure to one of the cornerstones of modern democracies –
the rule of law.[370]

C. The International Control Council - Iraq

There will be roles for the International community operating through the International
Military Tribunal, individual nations operating under the direct supervision of an
international body and for Iraqi domestic courts and commissions. These roles must be
harmonized, however, to ensure consistency and compliance with the rule of law. They also
must be coordinated in a fashion to maximize efficiency in an inherently inefficient process.
This is the role of a Control Council.

This Control Council will ideally be established under the auspices of the United
Nations[371] Security Council and given broad latitude to develop regulations governing both
the reconstruction of Iraq and more specifically the oversight of a post-conflict system of
justice. Such a system could be developed within the framework proposed by the United
States to the United Nations Security Council in which the United States and the United
Kingdom would manage the occupation and reconstruction of Iraq under the authority

---

[370] Some may argue that the best forum for accountability would be to turn the suspected war criminals over to
an international tribunal established in a far off land such as The Hague. While the idea of setting up a single
international body to try all such criminals is a noble one, it is doomed to provide at best an incomplete solution.
While it could serve as a method in which to bring justice to a selected few, it would fail to provide in method
of coordination among the various forums that will be necessary to fully meet the ends of justice, peace and
reconciliation in a nation where atrocities were common and committed potentially at the hands of many.

[371] If United Nations participation is blocked by malfeasance on the part of various Security Council members,
then it could be executed under the broad participation of the nations who pledged support for Operation Iraqi
Freedom.

established by a Security Council resolution.[372] The Council membership should be selected, as such, from nominations submitted to representatives of the United States and Great Britian from member nations involved in the liberation of Iraq as well as from member nations that have been subjected to Iraqi Aggression. A Chairman selected from the Council's membership should lead Control Council. The Chairman should be vested with executive authority and should be accountable to the Security Council itself.

As discussed above, the prosecution of war criminals by the International Military Tribunal at Nuremberg as well as by national military commissions was internationalized and placed under the ultimate control of the Control Council. This model, though expanded to meet the unique contingencies within Iraq, will provide the best forum from which to manage various matters such as to pretrial detention of suspected war criminals, the development of fundamental procedural and evidentiary norms of the various international courts, commissions and tribunals, and ultimately the resolution of disputes by competing constituencies. It can also serve to establish an appellate chamber for cases coming out of the International Military Tribunal and the various national commissions. In the early stages of the development of the Iraqi domestic courts, it could also oversee the development of their rules and procedures. Lastly, the Control Council, or one of its subdivisions, could

---

[372] Mark Turner, *Few dissent as US seeks approval at the UN for occupation*, FIN. TIMES, at 3. This proposal will provide for unity of command and also permit the process to continue as necessary in one year blocks of time following "an initial period of 12 months." *Id.*

serve as the final approval authority for verdicts and sentences meted out by the IMT or any

of the "internationalized" national military commissions.[373]

1. The International Control Council and Prisoner of War Repatriation

Apart from developing the basic ground rules for the prosecution of war criminals by the

international community, the Control Council should become heavily involved in the

repatriation process of any POWs held by the Allied parties to the conflict. As it is unlikely

that the various nations involved in the conflict will be aware of who is a potential war

criminal and who is simply a common soldier, coordination with the Control Council should

be required as part of the repatriation process. Further, this should be required of both

suspected war criminals and those whose participation in war crimes is unknown to the

nation detaining the POW. Suspected war criminals as well as the names of POWs should be

reported to the Control Council for screening. Further, the Control Council should

promulgate regulations that permit the placement of a detainer on the prisoner of war with

custody and control transferring to the Control Council upon repatriation.

Under this proposed structure, even if the United States held a prisoner that was

suspected to be a war criminal of specific interest to the United States, the Control Council

would have the primary authority and responsibility to place a detainer on the person in

---

[373] This is not to suggest that it should review or approve cases arising from the domestic courts except to the extent that it serves to meet its coordinating function. Once a case is placed in the hands of a domestic court, it should remain there except to the extent that it becomes apparent that the case was conducted as a sham to protect the wrongdoer from international accountability. The coordinating process discussed above, however, should minimize the likelihood of such action.

question and take them under their control at repatriation. At that point, the Control Council would evaluate the various forums available for prosecution and entertain requests for jurisdiction. At all times, however, the United Nations through its sanction of the Interim Authority managed by the United States and the United Kingdom and its organs such as the Control Council would maintain the responsibility for the control of the detainee.[374] Further, such release to this organ of the United Nations would not be a sham as it would create a responsibility for the Control Council to care for the detainee while removing the detainee from the control of the nation from which he was repatriated. Thus, the detainee ceases to be a prisoner of war at the hands of an individual nation, but a repatriated Iraqi now subject to detention pending trial by a United Nations sanctioned organ of the international community.

If the Control Council elects not to detain an individual, or the respective nation elects not to repatriate the suspect in question, then the nation that held the individual as a POW could elect to exercise jurisdiction over the suspected war criminal. Under these circumstances, such a prosecution would by definition fall outside of the control of the United Nations and would be governed by domestic and international law as it relates to the prosecution of criminals charged while held as a prisoner of war.[375] This is in contrast to

---

[374] Once the prisoner of war is repatriated and detained by the United Nations through its organ in Iraq, the Control Council, the detainee would lose his status as a prisoner of war for the purposes of Geneva Convention III. For the purposes of this convention, a prisoner of war is a person who meets certain requirements "who have fallen into the power of the enemy." Geneva Convention Relative to the Treatment of Prisoners of War, *opened for signature* Aug. 12, 1949, 6 U.S.T. 3316, 75 U.N.T.S. 135 (entered into force Oct. 21, 1950). They cease to be prisoners of war upon their "release and repatriation." *Id.* art. 5. Upon election of the United Nations to detain the individual, it would be difficult to conceptualize the individual as a prisoner of war held by the "enemy." Regardless, if the United States or another nation were to subsequently petition the Control Council for jurisdiction to prosecute before a national commission, the individual in question would not be a prisoner of the "enemy" at that time as they would be under the detained custody and control of the international community, not the United Nations.

[375] *See generally id.*

119

prosecutions before national courts that have been internationalized by their relationship to the Control Council and who are thus functioning under the authority of the United Nations.

2. The International Control Council and the Implementation of International Norms

The Control Council will be the representative of the international community on the ground. It will ideally be an instrumentality of the Security Council or its designated representatives. As such, it will have as a primary responsibility the development of the essential guidelines for the development of the rules of procedure and evidence for international courts established in Iraq. These guidelines would govern both the International Military Tribunal and the various underlying national commissions undertaken to extend the reach of the international community. It is by this process of control by regulation of the appellate process and by the act of final review that the Control Council serves as a mechanism from which to internationalize the operation of otherwise national commissions.

Within this environment, the Control Council will serve to enforce articulated international norms that it will codify for the purposes of its work from existing positive and customary international law. It will not, however, serve to regulate extensively the procedures utilized by the national courts to meet these basic norms. With respect to the procedures of the Court, the Control Council should ensure that all accused before the IMT in Iraq and various commissions at a minimum have the right to competent and conflict free counsel, access to evidence upon which the prosecution is based, the opportunity to interview before trial and to confront at trial witnesses presented against them and a detailed bill of particulars.

One such source for international norms is the International Covenant on Civil and Political Rights (ICCPR). The United Nations, through its agents such as the Control Council, should ensure that the systems developed for use in Iraq comply with its terms.[376] For example, while many nations oppose the death penalty, it may be imposed consistent with the ICCPR "for the most serious crimes."[377] If the death penalty is utilized for only serious crimes such as directing or committing murder, whether it be by sword or chemical bomb, the key provisions of the ICCPR will not be violated as Iraq continues to practice the death penalty and has not ratified the Second Optional Protocol to the ICCPR that prohibits executions "within the jurisdiction of a State Party."[378] Thus, as long as the trials are conducted within the territory of Iraq, or the territory of another nation that has not ratified the Second Optional Protocol to the ICCPR, the death penalty may be carried out by an international court consistent with existing treaty obligations.

Further, any attempt to divest the International Tribunal of the ability to impose the death penalty will set the stage for downstream consequences that will be unjust. Iraq will most likely desire to continue the death penalty, and nations such as the United States may have

---

[376] International Covenant on Civil and Political Rights of 16 December 1966, *at* http://www.unhchr.ch/html/menu3/b/a_ccpr.htm (entered into force Mar 23, 1976) [hereinafter ICCPR].

[377] *Id.* art. 6.

[378] Second Optional Protocol to the International Covenant on the Civil and Political Rights, aiming at the abolition of the death penalty of 15 December 1989, *at* http://www.unhchr.ch/html/menu3/b/a_opt2.htm [not entered into force) [hereinafter ICCPR Protocol II].

jurisdiction to try some potential war criminals in a United States District Court where there could be the potential for a death sentence. As such, an International Tribunal established to bring justice to the major war criminals should have the ability to provide punishments consistent with what lesser war criminals might face ultimately before national courts and commissions or the Iraqi domestic courts.

With respect to rules operating within the courtroom, strict adherence to traditional evidentiary rules developed in the common law tradition should not be required. Though the prosecutors should be permitted to relax these traditional rules, if such an election is made, the same relaxed standards should be made available to the defense. Lastly, the Control Council in their regulations should affirmatively state that the relaxed rules of evidence do not serve to relax the standards of proof in the case. It shall be up to the Tribunal and the lesser commissions to decide the weight that it desires to give to any particular evidence, if any. However, before any conviction is returned there must be a requirement that the evidence provided prove guilt beyond a reasonable doubt.[379]

3. The International Control Council, Competing Jurisdiction and Appeals

As discussed above, the Control Council should be used as the final arbiter of disputes over the forum utilized in any given prosecution. The POW repatriation-detainer process that

---

[379] The lessons from both the international tribunals and the military commissions after World War II provide that a just tribunal may utilize relaxed rules of evidence. The key to success is providing for proof beyond a reasonable doubt. *See supra* notes 225-290 and accompanying text. This will help to ensure the legitimacy of the forum's findings as well as the court's legitimacy. Even the horribly flawed International Criminal Court guarantees an individual the promise of conviction only upon the establishment of guilt beyond a reasonable doubt. *See* Rome Statute, *supra* note 26, art. 66(3).

all national armies and international forces will be required to follow facilitates this control. Once the Control Council has the suspected war criminal in its custody, it will evaluate the suspect for possible prosecution before the International Military Tribunal. In most cases, however, such individuals will fall below the jurisdiction of the IMT. In such cases, the individual will be available for prosecution by other internationalized bodies such as national courts operating under the auspices of the Control Council or by domestic courts, as appropriate. When confronted by competing requests, the Control Council will be responsible for determining which forum will have primary jurisdiction. In reaching its determination, the Control Council should weigh the competing interests of justice, the need to restore peace among the former belligerents, and reconciliation.

The Control Council can also utilize its position to identify suspects worthy of prosecution but who fall below the jurisdiction of the IMT. In some cases, there may not be an individual nation with a palpable interest in the prosecution of the individual at hand. Under these circumstances, the Control Council could request the assistance of one of the national courts that might be suitable for such a prosecution. For example, Iraq appears to have utilized jailed individuals as test subjects as part of their biological weapons program. While there may be no particular nation with a specific interest in prosecuting the scientists involved, the Control Council could evaluate such cases and request that a specific nation investigate and prosecute the matter as appropriate. This procedure would allow the Control

Council to make use of available forums with the necessary expertise to handle cases of varying complexity.[380]

The Control Council should also be responsible for establishing the standards for an independent appellate court. The court should be the sole appellate authority from all of the internationalized commissions as well as from the IMT in Iraq. Though the Control Council should be responsible for establishing the procedures and scope of review for the Court, the jurists could be selected by the Secretary-General of the United Nations from a list of nominees provided by the Security Council or the Control Council itself. This appellate court should be limited in function to ensure factual sufficiency of the findings and compliance with the standards required of all internationalized courts operating under the auspices of the Control Council. After the conclusion of the appeal process, the Control Council will serve as the final approval authority with convictions and punishments approved unless a majority of the members of the Council vote to set aside the conviction or mitigate the punishment.

Lastly, the Control Council should establish a domestic commission under the oversight of the domestic courts and the ultimate supervision of the Control Council to aid in the resolution of disputes related to the Arabization program.[381] This body should be utilized to

---

[380] For example, if the Iraqi government is determined to have conducted medical experiments, a national commission from a country with a well developed criminal system accustomed to handling forensically complicated cases could be of great assistance. Also, lessons from past practice such as in the *Medical Cases, United States v. Brandt, et al.*, I-II Tr. Of War Crim bef. the Nuernberg Mil. Trib. 1 (1947), *supra notes* 206-224 and accompanying text, may be helpful.

[381] *See supra* notes 327-341 and accompanying text.

resolve the various property disputes that will arise after the fall of the Hussein regime as various repopulated peoples begin to return to their traditional homelands. Such a system should be empowered to fix property rights and pay restitution to others who lose their home in the process.[382]

VII. Conclusion

The Twentieth Century, like many before it, was a century shaped by war. The Twentieth Century, unlike earlier eras learned the horrors of world wars waged in a manner in which planning and mobilization times were compressed followed by lethal and lightning fast conflict. Civilians moved from being in the position of hearing the distant thunder of cannons on the battlefield to being the subject of atrocities by tyrants bent on genocide and world conquest. The wars of the last century have provided the basis for the international body of law aimed at discouraging the potential wars of the future.

War is an inevitability. Civilized society, however, must be able to deter through collective force those who wish to wage illegal wars while strengthening the institutions that can spring into existence to punish the wrongdoer. The ultimate goal of these institutions must be the restoration of peace and the reconciliation of parties to the hostilities. Deterrence is another laudable goal, but it is questionable whether the fear of prosecution will ever deter

---

[382] People have been removed from their traditional homelands and moved all over Iraq by the Hussein government. As such, people are currently living in homes lived by others forced to move over the last decade. *See supra* notes 338-341.

the determined tyrant. Accordingly, the lessons of the past point to a model for the future. The model is one of flexibility and limited scope and duration.

All wars bring their distinct flavor of atrocities. Standing courts of international universal jurisdiction are inflexible and prone to politicization. Further, an attempt by individual nations to exercise jurisdiction over those whom they perceive as war criminals but with whom they have little or no direct relationship sets the stage for the tyranny of the minority. Neither contributes substantially to the process of peace or reconciliation and both have the potential for encouraging or extending hostilities.

An *ad hoc* system as the one discussed above for Iraq is a more appropriate model for Iraq and beyond. Rather than attempting to develop a "cookie cutter" approach, this system leverages the precedents of the past and the law of the day while providing a *system* tailored to meet the needs of reconciliation, peace and justice. Such a system is inherently reflective in nature, and the jurists brought together from a variety of backgrounds will force a more conservative approach to resolving the legal issues presented. Such a system will strive for legitimacy in the cases at hand knowing that their work is key to the reconciliation of the belligerents and a lasting peace. Such jurists will also be aware that history will judge it based on their response to the facts and cases they confront. They will seek legitimacy, accountability and justice, not the expansion of international law. International law will, therefore, inch forward at a pace tolerable to the international community, as opposed to racing forward like a run away train losing its respect and legitimacy as it goes.

The problems facing Iraq in the wake of the collapse of Hussein' regime are myriad and complex. Their resolution will be difficult and at times painful. Nonetheless, if hope can be restored the Iraqi people will be the ultimate beneficiaries. While the ultimate success in the reconstruction of Iraq will be in the hands of the Iraqi people, the international community can help shape the institutions that might bring the Iraqis peace and stability. The development of an equitable system of justice will further this goal while adding another brick for all to see to the foundation of the rule of law.

www.ingramcontent.com/pod-product-compliance
Lightning Source LLC
Chambersburg PA
CBHW080816180526
45168CB00006B/2464